How
I Coached
My Team to
Victory

JOHN SCHUCHARD

How I Coached My Team to Victory

ANGUS
& ROBERTSON
PUBLISHERS

ANGUS & ROBERTSON PUBLISHERS

Unit 4, Eden Park, 31 Waterloo Road,
North Ryde, NSW, Australia 2113 and
16 Golden Square, London W1R 4BN,
United Kingdom

First published in Australia
by Angus & Robertson Publishers in 1987

Copyright © John Schuchard, 1987

National Library of Australia
Cataloguing-in-publication data.

Schuchard, John, 1932–   .
*   How I coached my team to victory.*
*   Bibliography*
*   ISBN 0 207 15399 X.*
1. Soccer — Coaching. 2. Soccer — Psychological
*   aspects. I. Title.*
796.334'07'7

Typeset in 11/13 pt English Times by
Midland Typesetters Pty Ltd
Printed in Singapore

CONTENTS PAGE

INTRODUCTION

This is the true story of an amazing experience in applied psychology, a story of failure and success with an incredible (I won't keep it a secret a moment longer) result. Victory! An experience in the applied psychology of winning that resulted in actually winning!

Winning can be learned! And coordinating a group so that the members cooperate with each other to win is a skill that can be transmitted. But there is no simple formula involved. If it were, then the simple formula would be everywhere and everyone would be back to square one, all games would be drawn, and we would need another new formula. It is not quite like that.

If, while you are reading this book, you put it down and stare into space thinking about what happened, you might just find yourself in the same mental frame that I found myself in. I wish you luck.

The book tells you how to influence a group of players to win a game by saying the *right thing* to the team at the *right time*. There are a thousand ways to hit the jackpot and this is one of them. It is about what the coach said to the team every week, both when they lost and when they won. Put aside your Freud, your Jung, your Doctor Spock, your Hite Report, find a comfortable couch and read about applied psychology that works.

Warning: Parts of the book taken out of context can cause disasters, lost games, poison the atmosphere, work counter-productively and give me a bad name. The Team System is not a catch phrase that can be summed up in a clever word or two. So please read the whole book. It is not just the winning games that have information in them. The losing games are just as important. They are treated more briefly than the winning games because losing all the time is boring as well as being depressing. Some losing game strategies contain aspects that at first glance seem reasonable and rational—but don't work. Thirty absolute disasters.

The story starts about five years ago.

BOOK I
GAMES 1 TO 30

BOOK 1
GAMES 1 TO 30

Game 1
FIRST MATCH: DON'T DEMONSTRATE

Autumn was in the air and I noticed that the trees in the garden were turning golden-brown as I turned the last corner for home after work. The time was around 6 pm. I got out of the car and walked up the steps and in the back door.

"Hello, darling." Kiss. "Jim wants to play soccer."

My immediate reaction was, "Oh, God." I said, "Don't they play soccer at school?"

"No, only rugby."

I thought about it. I found the whole idea quite disgusting. I thought about football of all sorts in the same way as I thought about boxing! People maiming each other for fun. Well, if the alternative was rugby, I thought I had better settle for soccer. At least foul play was penalised (I had watched soccer on television) whereas with rugby foul play seemed to be the way to win the game.

Within a week Jim and I were in the car, driving to the local playing fields. It was a midweek day and I had left work early.

Let me explain my attitude. I was educated in Victoria, Australia, where the main game of football is called Australian Rules. I was made to play a total of about three games. I was so bad I was not chosen again and I thought that would be the end of it. I was shunted off to play other sports on sports day every week.

And now my son wanted to get into the action. My ideas had not changed a lot since schooldays. I saw football as a war in miniature. There were two sides and the fighters did not actually get killed. But almost. The spectators not only enjoyed the sight of the mock killing but frequently emulated the soldiers on the field and turned on each other in the grandstands with fists and beer bottles and cans, both full and empty (the bottles, the cans *and* the spectators).

Real blood seemed to flow in the grandstands as it did on the field. I read about it in the newspapers. The facts all seemed quite plain. It was obvious that the most aggressive team won the game. I think it was Rudyard Kipling who said it is not whether you win or lose the game that counts, but how you play it. No problem for me. I hated the playing, and I hated watching.

While I had never actually won I found the syndrome of "win, win, win" nauseating. Win what? There was nothing to win. There might be some trophy, but anyone could buy a trophy. I decided that the real thrill must be in putting down the losing team. It was all quite depressing.

And now my own son wanted to play soccer. Where had I gone wrong? I had failed to teach him the proper values of life and now he had some kind of blood lust. He may just as well have said he wanted to take up violent crime.

We arrived at the local grounds with about an hour of daylight left. Later, when it grew dark, bright overhead lights were switched on, illuminating the whole field, which was covered with people, most of them boys. Hundreds of them. And standing taller than the boys were dozens of adult leaders in their uniforms of track suits. It looked, well, fascist. They had clipboards and were taking names. It looked like World War III preparations. Dozens of teams were being formed.

I knew a few of the adults and said hello.

"John," I heard, and through the crowd came my good friend Harry Radds. "John," said Harry, "how about taking a team of the younger kids and teach them soccer?"

"Harry, you must be joking." I told him that not only had I never played the game but I was the last person in the world to coach soccer. "The nearest I have ever come to soccer is watching it on TV."

Harry said, "Please. Why not give it a go? The fact is, we just don't have enough coaches."

"Sorry. No."

"Please. Look, you don't have to know anything about soccer. If you could just supervise them kicking the ball around."

"Sorry."

"OK, well how about just for the time being. And as soon as we get more coaches I'll replace you. Please. Fred over there will fix you up with some kids and gear. Good man. Great. See you later . . ."

By the time Jim and I headed home an hour later, I had a list of about a dozen kids. I was to be their minder. But just for the time being.

One week later I went into a city department store and looked at track suits. I tried some on and chose a blue one with white stripes down the sleeves and down the sides of the trousers. I put it on and looked in the mirror. I looked like either an astronaut or a Grand Prix racing driver. I held my stomach in and stuck my chest out. I felt extremely embarrassed, took off the track suit, paid for it and took it home. Time would not stand still for me.

Training night arrived, right on schedule. Jim and I drove to the field.

I introduced myself to a few people and held my list of boys and wandered around, wondering how I would find them. It got dark and the lights came on. For about an hour I got progressively more nervous, but I finally found myself addressing most of the boys on my list.

I kept telling myself I was an art director, not a youth leader.

I had four soccer balls, but not the faintest idea what I should do with them. I told the boys to kick the balls about and to each other. They promptly kicked a couple of balls into the bushes where it was completely dark, and they followed them into the darkness and out of sight. They were not the slightest bit interested in doing anything other than mucking up.

A man wrote down my name and gave me all sorts of paraphernalia from the soccer club. Including a first-aid kit! I thought, My God, it is for real. They actually do expect to maim each other. What have I let myself in for?

HOW I COACHED MY TEAM TO VICTORY

I was given the club shirts—one shirt for every player. The boys themselves provided pants (but these shorts were "regulation" and all looked the same), and soccer boots and shin guards. Shin guards!! Fibreglass shields so that their shins would not get smashed in the game. So they wouldn't get crippled by another boy kicking them. I was given a few more soccer balls, a few bits and pieces and a list of games to be played. One of the bits was a bucket, another a sponge. Another was a bandage and the sight of that bandage made me think long and hard about what I was doing. Was I going to war; but because of some religious belief not shooting the guns, but merely driving the ambulance?

I looked at the list. It listed dates and times and the names of suburbs nearby. The names of the suburbs were the names of the teams from those suburbs. The thought of escorting this group of children to a nearby "village" to play against the local lads was unbelievable.

In spite of my prayers the weekend arrived. I had organised—with about ten phone calls—the players to get to the ground. Some travelled alone, some picked up other players whose parents did not come. Saturday morning we set off for a nearby suburb, and there was the soccer field with the nets for goals at each end. I looked around and saw the most likely-looking type for a sports coach. I was looking for a man in a track suit. I, of course, was wearing my blue one. I introduced myself to him. We showed each other our lists of players. These included pictures like passport photographs of each player, and their names. I think the idea was so that nobody could "ring in" an advanced or older player.

I forget which team it was, but I don't forget how I felt. I just wished I was elsewhere. Anywhere. It seemed that circumstances had pushed me into something that I not only could not do, but actually knew was bad for people. Where would it lead? Little did I know then what a metamorphosis my outlook would undergo.

Well, I could have anticipated the result of the game. We were going to lose it, of course! I knew this fact before the game even started. Did I think I was Attila the Hun? I felt more like mild-mannered Clark Kent with no Superman suit or phone booth handy.

Well, the lads put on their team shirts and ran onto the field. The whistle blew and the game commenced. We got beaten five goals to none. We were quite hopeless. And we certainly were not going to learn any aggression. All we were going to learn was defeat.

Two teams — all young boys — one lot in one colour and the other lot in a different colour. Twenty minutes in one direction, a short rest and then 20 minutes in the other direction and the ordeal was over for us. Games for adults go for 45 minutes each "half". For these boys each half was shortened to 20 minutes.

We had lost. We lost quite naturally. Predictably. It was the easiest thing in the world to do. We were incompetent. I say *we* lost, although my feelings at the time were that *they* — the team of which I was the coach — lost. I certainly was not on the field playing. They were playing for themselves and presumably they were playing as well as they could. I remember wondering at the time whether or not they had enjoyed themselves.

That night I rang my friend Harry. I told him how hopeless it all was, and he said he would do his best to find someone else to take over the team. I said, "Yeah, well Harry, the sooner the better because I really don't like it at all."

"How did you go?" said Harry.

"We lost five-nil," I said.

Silence. "Look, I'll see what I can do," said Harry.

Almost beyond belief, three days later, midweek, there I was at the playing field at what I laughingly called soccer training. It was, frankly, ludicrous. I don't know why I did not just flatly refuse to go and to hell with the boys. It was a repeat of the first week.

I don't know quite what got into me that week. But one lunchtime found me browsing through a bookstore. There I was, looking at books about soccer. There wasn't any possibility that I was wrong, that it was not really a kind of war. That it brought out the very worst in people . . . was there? I bought some books on how to play the game.

The training session lasted an hour and a half. The kids were mucking up most of the time. They were not really interested in the finer points and the techniques and skills that I had swotted up on. I had bits of paper with diagrams on them showing how to train and how to kick the ball and so on. The moment of truth came when I said, "Pay attention everyone. Here is how to kick the ball into the net. This is how to score a goal."

I placed the ball on the ground. They all watched. I took two paces back and stepped forward and kicked the ball. I looked in horror as it sailed clear over the top of the net and bounced off a car in the car park and landed near another group training further down the field. Embarrassed out of my mind I ran and asked for our ball back. I thought of asking one of the boys to fetch it but went myself just to get away from them for a minute. When I brought it back I could tell they all thought the same about their coach. Incompetent. It was my first experience of what I would call a really bad group look. I was to see it often.

On the spot I thought up my first rule for coaching. It is a rule I have not modified. I don't necessarily recommend it, but for me it is iron-clad: *never, ever demonstrate "live"*. By "live" I mean as though in a game. That one embarrassing moment taught me that if I wished to demonstrate something I had better develop a method that did not make me look like an absolute fool.

I tried to compose myself in front of the smirking group. I placed the ball on the ground to demonstrate a kick that would go into the net. In slow motion I moved my foot back and got everybody to notice the angle of my foot. Then I asked the biggest kid to come forward and kick the ball as hard as he could, using the tips I had just given him. (I did know some of the physics involved and I had swotted up a bit from the notes that the club had given the coaches.)

I glanced at the group. They were all watching! Lesson number one. Lesson to me that is. They all knew I was not worth watching but one of their mates was a different thing.

The ball shot like a bullet into the net. I decided the coaching lurk would not take too long to master. No demonstrations — get the players themselves to do all the demonstrations. I was on the right track, but just a bit naive. (I was 30 games and 30 training sessions of hard work and apprenticeship premature.)

We played around for an hour and at last parents arrived to take their sons home. I took my son home, showered, ate, and thought. Harry had not replaced me as he said he would. But on the other hand I wouldn't repeat the embarrassment bit (I thought) since I had worked out how to avoid it. Little did I know.

Game 2

BIOGRAPHY

I am by occupation an art director in a graphic arts company. In my mind's eye I look like Woody Allen. (The "look" is more mental than physical.) Although as a child I was reasonably good at some sports, I didn't particularly like football because I found it too brutal. I still think — even now that I've moved from Victoria — that Australian Rules is an awkward game because of the shape of the ball. It bounces irregularly (being elongated like a rugby ball) so that the players scrambling for the ball always look awkward. They cannot tell which way it is going to bounce and it always bounces very unevenly and in unexpected directions. Arms scoop up the ball and any precision seems impossible. It is not quite my style.

The only ball game I played was tennis. I liked balls to be spherical and bounce predictably. Tennis had the true game aspect in that it was as much fun playing *with* a friend as *against* him. But in football — as in boxing — it seemed to be necessary to hate the opposition. I never hated anyone I played tennis with or against.

For the same reason rugby never really took my fancy and, as well, rugby seemed much more violent than Australian Rules football. A friend of mine is a front row forward for a First Division rugby team. His name is Geoff. I said to Geoff one day, "Don't you feel any sense of responsibility about the violence in rugby?"

He looked amazed. "Absolutely not!"

"But guys get their spines broken playing rugby. If you hold a player around the waist upside down and spear him into the ground, well of course you are going to snap his spine," I said.

Geoff thought about it. He said, "Actually, yes we do turn them upside down and spear them into the ground, but there's no need for it. They don't need to have their spines broken at all."

I said, "Paraplegics!"

"It's terribly, terribly easy to avoid," said Geoff. "All they have to do is give me the ball and I won't break their spines at all. I don't want to hurt anybody. I just want the ball!" He smiled broadly. "Look, do you want to know how to win a game of football?" (He meant rugby.)

"How?"

"Well, in the first ten minutes you have to frighten the daylights out of the opposition team." (Except he didn't say "daylights", he said something nastier.) "After that you have an easy game." The smile was like a friendly tiger's.

That seems to sum up rugby to my mind. One of the things I had noticed about the fathers of the guys in our soccer team was that many were ex-rugby players who appreciated that soccer is a non-violent game. Their own rugby experiences had been too violent to wish on their sons.

Soccer is a game of skill, and violence is theoretically not a part of the game. Violent play is penalised with a free kick to the opposition. So a player with the ball at his feet attempts to run away from an opponent rather than smash him to the ground or smash him out of the way. My knowledge of soccer was gained from watching televised matches of English and German teams and once, in England, watching a live game.

A few years ago I was in England visiting my in-laws in Scarborough. I went to London one Saturday and (by arrangement) met my good friend Harry Radds who was in England at the time. We caught the tube train to Highbury and we watched Arsenal play Manchester United. The ground was full, and we recognised most of the players from seeing them on television. The atmosphere was electric. No violence at that game.

We found ourselves in the midst of Arsenal supporters, the home team. The Manchester United fans are notorious for smashing up the place if their team loses but they were well-behaved that Saturday. It was a rare experience for me. The game finished with the score at a draw — one goal each.

Back in Sydney, game 2 came along. Nothing could stop it. It was an "away" game with cars full of players and their parents arriving at the ground. They all parked in the parking lot, gathered around and greeted each other. They took a couple of balls and kicked them about. It is called "warming up". One of our players said to me, "They are not a very good team. We might even play to a drawn game if we're lucky."

I don't remember my response but I do remember thinking about what he had said. It seemed strange. Surely he would be thinking, "They're not much of a team, that means we can *win* today." But no. The best he could think of was a draw. I puzzled over it. In fact for nearly 30 games I puzzled over it.

We played the first half, we ate oranges at half-time, and we played the second half. We lost two nil. We got into our cars and we all drove home. It was depressing. Both games we had played we had lost. Oh, well, I thought. Maybe next week. Had I known I was destined to lose 30 games in a row I would have driven over a cliff and ended it all there and then. But hope springs eternal. I drove home with my son.

Game 3
RULES OF THE GAME

There are many books on the game of soccer. Briefly, the game is played on a rectangular field and at the start each team stands in its respective half.

There are 11 players in each team (see over). Number 1 is the goalkeeper. He may pick up the ball with his hands but not run with it. He must throw it or kick it. Outside his marked box he may not handle it but must play as any other player, and not touch the ball with his hands. All the other players may kick the ball, but not touch it with their hands. If they do, it is a free (standing) kick to the other team. They may bounce the ball off their bodies — chest, head, etc. Goalies are a rare breed of player, usually very talented, brave individuals.

Players 2, 3 and 4 are the "backs". They must keep their cool, be highly disciplined and are normally facing the ball and wishing to kick it in the general direction from whence it came — away from the goal they are defending. They must ideally have a high level of body language (or spoken) so that they do not misunderstand each other at a critical moment and let a goal through their defences. They must form a team within a team. They must be able to spread out across the field running away from their goal and render an opposition player "offside" at a critical moment in the play. When they do that they have to leave no other players defending their goal other than their lonely goalkeeper. So they must have nerves of steel as well as other skills.

Players 5, 6 and 7 are the "midfield" players. Their particular skill requirements are to take the ball and pass it to one of their forwards. (Two famous midfield players are

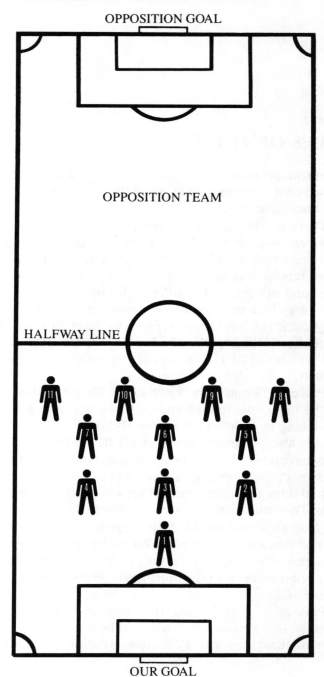

OPPOSITION GOAL

OPPOSITION TEAM

HALFWAY LINE

OUR GOAL

Franz Beckinbauer and Glen Hoddle.) Long accurate kicks are often their specialty.

Players 8, 9, 10 and 11 are the "forwards" or "strikers". Their job is to score the goals. Of course anybody (except a goalie) can score a goal from anywhere on the field, but the strikers should score the most. Strikers are often inventive and idiosyncratic. Some are super fast runners over a distance of ten metres. Some are incredibly quick at twisting and turning. Some are skilled at putting a lot of spin onto a ball as they kick it, resulting in the ball curving through the air, or floating like a frisbee.

These positions are not part of the rules of the game, simply a conventional approach to a "starting point" for organising tactical manoeuvres. The rules state that players can be anywhere in their half of the field before play commences. Any pattern of players is possible but playing without a pattern usually results in losing.

The main rules are very reasonable. If a player kicks the ball out of bounds then the other team has the throw-in from the boundary line. If a player touches the ball with his hands the other team gets a free kick. Any free kick is awarded to the team as a whole and any player on the team can take the free kick. If an attacking team kicks the ball over the back line the defending goalkeeper gets a free kick. If a defending player kicks the ball back out over his own defence line then the other (attacking) team gets to kick the ball in from the corner of the field. If a player commits a foul, such as tripping or punching, the other team gets a free kick.

The Offside Rule is different from all the other rules. Briefly, a player cannot receive a "forward pass" if there are no opposition (defending) players between him and the goal, not counting the defending goalkeeper. So if the defenders form a line across the field, the attackers must first kick the ball past that line and only then may they attack from a position in between all the opposition players and their goal. A soccer rule book will provide the definitive explanation.

Training session number three was two hours, going into the night with lights on the field because winter was coming on. The guys were kicking the ball around. My job was organising little games—not games of soccer, but games designed to heighten the skill of the players. All the best teams in the world start out doing this sort of thing (I found out!).

For instance, line the players up in two parallel lines and have them kick the ball across to each other without kicking it so hard that it misses everybody. When the players feel like misbehaving they easily kick the ball into the bushes and out of sight. Then they disappear into the night. If they are behaving, then the game is to sharpen up accurate kicking over a fairly short distance.

Another game is for everybody to form a large circle and face the centre, with one player in the middle. The object of the game is for the players in the ring not to let the player in the middle get the ball. Whenever he rushes toward the ball, the player who has it kicks it sideways so in one way or another the player in the middle cannot keep up with it. When the player in the middle touches the ball the last player to kick it swaps places with him. There are a lot of games like that which are quite fun and heighten and extend the players' own skill and development. So I tried to train them.

Game 3, and we went and put on our club shirts. We ran onto the field, and we lost. Back at training session a few days later we practised kicking right over the top of the goal. We practised high kicking, low kicking, long kicking, short kicking and sideways kicking.

Game 4
GOODBYE FIRST TEAM

Game 4 we lost. I could see the players — although they seemed to enjoy the game even when they lost — thinking maybe they weren't very good. Well, I supposed they enjoyed it or they wouldn't have kept coming to the games. At least some of them enjoyed it. Some, however, were getting a bit depressed. One dropped out; he said he didn't want to play again.

We still had enough boys in the squad to pick out a team, but I was getting as depressed as the players. There were about 20 games in a season and I was getting pretty used to my team losing after only four games. Then, on a Sunday night, I got the call. It was Harry. He had found a coach.

"Fantastic," I said. "Thank God," I added. I did not even have to say goodbye to the team, all I had to do was deliver the gear to a local address, thus avoiding a lot of embarrassment. So that was that. The ordeal was over at last. I thought.

Game 5

HELLO SECOND TEAM

"John," said Harry's voice on the telephone. Not two weeks had gone by.

Like a sucker I said, "Yeah?"

"Look, I know what you said but one of our coaches has just shot through overseas. No notice, just gone. Could you please help out. Just for a little while. Just until we get someone . . . could you? Otherwise I don't know what I'll do."

How could I refuse? I kept racking my brains for a way. And so, hard to believe, down to training midweek. The new group. They looked just as recalcitrant as the first lot. They fooled about just as much. We did not get much training done beyond taking their names and having a bit of a soccer game with a neighbouring group on the field.

Saturday rolled along. Incredibly—we drew! The score was nil. A scoreless game. I can remember smiling at the new players. I was ecstatic, although I didn't show it. My best kept secret was that I had never coached a team to victory. As we said goodbye to each other and "See you at training", I shouted, "We'll do better next week." Perhaps I was not totally useless and incompetent.

Then the truth dawned. Wake up to yourself, John. They are better soccer players than the first team. That is it, nothing to do with coaching at all. Perhaps they will win a game or two. They had certainly enjoyed themselves more than the first team. Maybe I would have some fun after all.

Game 6

THE PURSUIT OF EXCELLENCE

We did some training in midweek which was not totally boring, and I changed my mind a little. They were not talented, but then again they were not hopeless. I guess they were average.

Game 6 came along. We went onto the field with a certain sparkle, but we lost. It crossed my mind that some of the teams that beat us were not particularly aggressive. But pleasant? My God, I thought, if they were pleasant they would let us win once in a while, something they never did. "They" being the opposition. They were all the same—none of them would let us win. Rotten sods.

Game 7

JUMP UP QUICKLY

"Last week I noticed that when some of you fell down you just stayed there. Well, don't. When you fall down, if you jump straight up again, quite often you will find that you can get back into the game, or maybe the game has moved away from you and then back near you! If you just lie there, as if you have given up, then the other team can take its time and line up a kick or just dribble the ball which ever way their players want to. So please try. Please."

They tried. But we lost.

Game 8

CONCENTRATE

At training I addressed them all. "Look, you guys. At the last game a lot of you were losing your concentration when the ball was up the other end, away from you. And then when the ball came flying down your way you were not ready for it. Now this is a team sport. It takes the whole team to play the game. If you are standing around—well, don't. Get ready for when the ball comes your way. OK?"

It was hard to say if they did what I had asked or not. Maybe they did. But game eight, we lost.

Game 9
TECHNICAL STRATEGIES

Before game nine I gathered the players around me and talked about strategy. "If the ball is down their end but at the side, I want to see at least two players move to a position in front of their goal ready for a kick in from the side."

This seemed to make sense to them.

"Now — strikers. When you see the ball moving down the side of the field and you can see a possible pass coming in from the side — move! Start heading for the goal and when the ball comes in, bang! You will be moving in ready for a kick into the net."

They did not seem to be thinking ahead of the game play at any particular moment. They were like children of fortune, following the ball and the game but not leading anywhere. We lost.

Game 10

PASS AHEAD OF YOUR TEAM-MATE

We had a practice session after game 9. I said, "Now if you line up a pass to your team-mate — don't pass it to him." This caused a little amazement. But I had their attention. I went on, "Pass it to where he will be!" I let that sink in for a few seconds. "If he is running forward and you pass the ball to where he is, then he is going to have to stop. Isn't he? So what you have to do is kick the ball to where he will be *when the ball arrives*."

I demonstrated by positioning players for the others to see. I pointed out where the goal was and placed two players about 15 paces apart and told them they were running towards the goal. I pointed to the place where the player with the ball should aim. We then set about practising the manoeuvre. The practice worked well. About half the time the ball went where it was meant to go. The receiving player did not always receive the ball properly, mostly I suspected because he was a little surprised at it actually arriving in front of him while he was still running. I went home that night feeling slightly confident. Would we really crack it this time? Would they finally get their act together?

They did not. We lost.

Game 11

TRAINING TECHNIQUES

All the coaches received a bundle of literature from the club. It was mostly on how to coach a team. I read it all. It was enlightening regarding some of the rules that I had not known about (although minor points) and advice on how to kick the ball and so on.

At training I looked at the pictures, showed them to the players, and together we worked through them. I knew not to demonstrate, and selected a player to demonstrate to the rest of the team a particular technique. It worked well and held their interest. As I was talking to them I realised that the glazed look of someone being lectured to (and being bored by the lecture) was coming over their eyes. But generally the group was quite happy.

Game 11. Some of the training may have got through! We drew the game one-all. They were pretty happy about it. It seemed much better than no score at all, and so much better than getting beaten.

Game 12

ABSENTEEISM

The team had had about half-a-dozen games, but no wins. The players had had some fun, but not a lot. Training after game 11 had been with about four players away.

Game 12 was an away game; about ten kilometres away. Five minutes before start of play we were still four players short of a team. I thought, I will find the opposition coach and tell him I'm very sorry but through sickness (or something) we are too short of players. Sorry, mate, but we will have to concede the game to you. Forfeit. And then, just as I was about to give up, two more of our players arrived.

Starting time. What to do? Nothing to do, we play with less players. Then I thought about asking the opposition coach would he mind playing two players short to make a more even game of it. He came over to me and — I could hardly believe it — he had actually counted our players! We exchanged player's cards and he said, "You're two players short. Tough luck. We had to play one short last week. Well, it's time to start." He was so authoritarian I could not even get up the nerve to ask him whether we could both play smaller teams to make a fairer game of it.

At half-time we were losing four to nil. I couldn't think of anything to say to the team. They tried valiantly in the second half but when the final whistle blew we had lost seven goals to our none. I seemed to be losing my grip on things. Not only were we losing every game but now I was losing players. I could see the nightmare of me arriving at a ground with the last two or three loyal players and losing 100 to nil.

I drove home very depressed.

Game 13

CALL FOR THE BALL

About two-thirds of the players turned up for training. I was too embarrassed to say anything about the small turn-up. I started a "lesson".

"Look," I said, "when one of you has the ball, the players who are in the clear — if you have no opposition players near you — call out for the ball. If Terry has the ball, call out '*Terry!*'. But you are not allowed to call out anything that could trick the opposition. Not permitted. For example, if the opposition has the ball you are not allowed to say, 'Here, pass it here!' pretending you are on his side. That would be a foul. Understand? So the safest thing is to call each other by name."

Game 13 was at our home ground. For most of the game the suburb resounded to the sounds of players' first names. Most of the players were calling out to other players throughout the game. Their enthusiasm was unbounded.

All the noise was in vain. Usual result, we lost.

Game 14

FATHER FELLS SON

Game 14 was to be played at a ground six kilometres away.

Ken was a Canadian player. He had red hair, was a nice guy and he had a very overbearing father. Ken's father, whose name was George, had to be seen to be believed. He was the most aggressive person you could imagine. He had played rugby in England and he knew the way to win a game: you simply smashed the opposition. Easy. If they didn't give you the ball, you tore their arms off. And George was raising his children to think the same way he did. Young Ken was too tall for his age, which made him awkward. He was probably the most uncoordinated kid on the team. He had a nice nature, but he wanted to please his father. And he did that by trying to be as aggressive as possible. How to win games was to kick shins. Simple.

We lost game 14, two to nil. Which made it a particularly forgettable game, except for one startling incident in the first half. It was to plant the seed in my mind that eventually grew into the system of applied psychology, the Team System. It was an incident that — 16 games later — was to be repeated in another form. It happened right in front of me.

I was standing about halfway along our half of the field at the sideline. I was not shouting much at anybody and play was almost equal between the two teams. The ball came down right in front of me where players engaged in a footwork duel to gain possession of it. There was no dirty play but three or four players from each side were quite near to each other and the ball was being kicked about like the ball in a pinball machine.

Ken was on the edge of the group on "our" side of all the

players. So he had every player in the group between him and the opposition goal. If he got the ball he either had to cut a swathe through the group or go around them. He got it, and his normal form would have been to smash his way through everyone — friend and foe — but this time he didn't. He twisted and turned and kept the ball at his feet, gently tapping it from one foot to the other. Then he headed off to go around the pack.

Unusual for him, not attacking directly. He usually used his height to intimidate the opposition, and when he charged players they tended to get out of his way. So for an instant the group did not move *en masse* towards him. They hesitated and waited to see which way the ball would go before committing themselves to running this way or that.

A second or so later he was moving away from the group, keeping the ball at his feet, but moving towards our own goal, in a kind of temporary retreat.

Ken's father, George, was standing at the sideline about ten paces from me. His loud Canadian voice bellowed out, "Kenneth, you're going the wrong goddamn way!"

About two seconds later Ken was lying on the ground, having fallen, and the ball was gone — over to the other side of the field and away from us. Other players had fallen as well, but they quickly jumped to their feet and were away and into the game. All the spectators were watching the ball and the state of play at the other side of the field.

Except me. I was staring at where Ken had fallen. Now, Ken was not the best coordinated player in the team. And players sometimes trip themselves up. But I had seen something that struck me as being abnormal. Ken had seemed to stiffen up before he fell, and I was quite positive that *no player had touched him*. I was sure he had tripped himself. Or had he? I turned and looked at his father, who was shouting at the play far away. And then I knew for sure. There was no doubt in my mind at all. Ken's father had tripped Ken up and he had done it with his voice. As surely as if he had swept his large athletic leg and knocked the boy's legs from under him he had brought his own son to the ground with his voice alone.

Ken had been concentrating on keeping the ball at his feet, and getting it away from the other players. He may well have lost his sense of direction, or he may have been planning to take the ball with him around the group and across the field. We'll never know. The avalanche of sound from his father went in Ken's ears, around in his brain, found its way to his neuromuscular motor controls and fouled up his leg coordination. Crash. Gravity had completed the job. The whole incident was over in about two seconds, but it seemed to freeze-frame in my mind's eye. And then, strange to say, the affair seemed to slip from my consciousness. I did not give it a single thought for months.

The game became exciting. Within a few minutes I had dismissed the incident as a nasty bit of behaviour on the part of Ken's father, but nothing more. The players played quite well, but we lost three to nil. We packed our gear, got into our cars and drove away. I didn't give a second glance at the place where Ken had fallen. I was not to think of it again for months. But when I did, I recalled it very clearly. I could hear Canadian George's voice ringing out, "Kenneth . . ."

Game 15
EVEN AT HALF-TIME

Game 15 started at a tremendous pace. I could not believe we were doing so well against such a good opposition. They were a much better team and yet our players went hell for leather and held their own. Our goalie made a few very good saves and then kicked the ball a long way down the field, and away we went, attacking.

It was a fast game. The ball seemed to fly from one end of the field to the other and back again. But no goals. Not one to anyone. The half-time whistle blew, and I was ready with the oranges. All our guys looked hot and flushed. They had played well and they were happy—they knew they were playing against a good team and they were proud of the score at nil-all.

I could not think of anything worth saying; they were doing well on their own and I thought that anything I said would sound a bit stupid. And then something happened that I was not immediately aware of.

The guys started talking to each other. Well, I thought, nothing the matter with that. Friends talking to each other. Talking while they sucked and chewed on their oranges.

One said, "My God those guys are big!" Another said, "You're not kidding!" A few others joined in and said how well we were doing against such a crack team. Another said, "Here, look at that," and showed a bruised leg. "One kicked me."

I said, "Do you mean on purpose?"

He said, "I don't suppose so, but they are a pretty rough lot." The whistle went for the second half. Still I did not realise what had happened.

But something had definitely happened. We were quite hopeless. If the ball came towards two players — one of ours and one of theirs — our player held back. The opposition player got control of the ball and only then did our player try to get the ball from him. And all our players were the same! They seemed hesitant. I would not call it frightened. When they tackled a player for the ball they were quite brave about it. But they obviously did not want to be the first to arrive at the ball itself. They all wanted the other team to actually get the ball and only then did they want to tackle them. It was strange indeed to watch, and very puzzling. Our players were not being "cowardly", but they were waiting for the opposition to make the first move each time. Also, our kicks became much less accurate, and there were a few other symptoms in our generally bad play. But the most obvious was this holding back and then joining in late.

We lost three goals in the second half. We scored none. We had talked ourselves into losing the game three to nil. Before the players had talked about the situation at half-time they were battling on bravely. As they talked about it they became more and more anxious. It was not until much later — maybe 15 games later — that I worked out what we had done. It seems so obvious now, but at the time it seemed like normal conversation, which would perhaps have bonded them in a kind of camaraderie, sharing a crisis. Not so. At the start of the half-time break I had been excited and proud. So, I am sure, were they. By the start of the second half they had psyched themselves into losing.

After the game I felt the usual rotten depression. I drove home.

Game 16
TEAM MANAGEMENT: RELIABILITY

At training I got talking to a successful coach while my team was kicking the ball around. He was talking about the programme for upcoming matches. He showed me his list. List? I had a list I had been given by the soccer club but it did not look anything like this one.

"Where did you get that great list?" I asked him.

"I made it out of the one they gave me," he said.

We talked some more. I was trying to see if there were any secrets to successful coaching that I could borrow. Making my own list was a start.

Next day at work I set out all the games for the rest of the season and rewrote them in a better format. The where, when and who of all games. I made a copy for each member of the team. Would efficiency with the paperwork help in winning games? Maybe if I was efficient at something then the players would listen to what I had to say about other things, and then when I said "please win" they would do it. I thought.

It didn't quite work out that way. We lost the game. But everybody still had their lists. So at least I didn't have to phone everybody each Friday night. And that was a workload gone and my Friday nights free. I went further. I resolved to be more efficient.

I got over my Hitler Youth Complex. I made sure I had all the things I needed every week, both for training night and for the games. Things like the match report. Things like the ball pumped up to the correct pressure, not too hard, not too soft. The paper work for game results and so on. Maybe efficiency was the answer to our appalling endless run of losing games.

Game 17
TEAM WITHIN A TEAM

I noticed that two or three players were fond of playing near each other. I guessed they were friends apart from soccer. I realised they were forming teams within the larger team. I viewed the situation with mild alarm! My immediate reaction was that they would compete with the rest of the team and not cooperate with other team members who were not part of their exclusive inner sanctum. That was surely the way to lose. If we could not have one coordinated team we had no hope at all.

So I broke them up. I placed them apart from each other. I was relieved when they did not complain, but did it alter our performance? It did not. We went down like a house of cards. At half-time we were two down. By the final whistle we had lost five to nil.

I went home confused. How on earth could a team function with sub-teams within it? I couldn't see how it was possible.

Game 18

GREAT AT TRAINING, HOPELESS AT THE MATCH

At training, about halfway through, I threw the ball up and the players headed it into the goal. Actually, I threw the ball up quite high and the players had to wait until it bounced, and then hit it with the front of their heads and (hopefully) into the net.

If you bounce the ball on the very top of your head it may hurt. The place to use is about at the top of the forehead, round about the front hairline. I learnt this from an experienced player and passed it on to my group. I stood at the side of the net and threw the ball about ten metres into the air. Each player tried once. Only one guy scored a goal. All the others missed. But the surprising thing was that the guy who scored was Michael.

He was the weakest kid in the team. The worst player and certainly the most frightened. He would turn and run away when the ball came near him on the soccer field. If there was nobody near him then he would kick the ball, but if there were any other players close to the ball — even from our own team — forget about Michael. I never noticed if his kicks were good or bad, I just chose to ignore him because he was such a bad player.

I said, "Once again everyone," and they lined up in a queue to head the ball. This time two other players scored goals — and Michael scored again. I said, "Well, Michael is the only guy that scored every time." Nobody turned to look at him. "Let's give it another try."

Again, Michael and several other players scored. The guy was obviously brilliant at heading the ball.

Michael's father was a big, aggressive man and the kid

himself was built like a feather. There was nothing to him. His arms and legs were like match sticks. If I had a build like that, I thought, I would be dead scared of all the players no matter whose team they were from. But, I thought, if I can only get him near the opposition goal with no other players around, and a high bouncing ball . . .

It happened. It really happened.

Game 18 was quite a good game. It was in the second half and we were two goals down, but we were playing well. We had the ball down near the opposition goal (which we had done more than half the time during the game) and we had Michael running forward. And we were given by the gods a high bouncing ball. Michael moved towards the goal, there were no imminent players going to smash him to the ground. He headed it. Right over the top of the net. No goal. Goal kick (a kick from the ground by their goalkeeper).

Hence the heading to this game. Here was a kid who was brilliant at training but hopeless at the game. I thought about it, accepted it, and that was that. It was as though it was a part of Michael's personality. Unchangeable, of course. We had a player who could show everyone how to do things at training. But in a real game he was a total embarrassment.

Looking back on the game, I can remember thinking that nothing could be done about it. It was a fact of life as was a player's weight or height. How could I have been so dumb?

Game 19

THE OTHER TEAM LOOKS TOUGH, SO PLAY HARD

We arrived at the game — six kilometres from home — and everybody looked full of beans. The guys kicked the ball around and put on their tops. I had arrived with a large Italian father, Luigi, and we had chatted about this and that, mostly small talk. It was a nice day and how was his wife and so on. And then he said an amazing thing to the group of players gathered around.

He said, "Now I've heard that the other team is pretty good so you will have to play hard today."

Everyone said, yeah, OK, we'll play hard, we're pretty tough ourselves, so what's new.

Amazing? Not at first hearing. A very ordinary conversation. But a little while later, when there were no players around, Luigi said to me with a little laugh, "Who are we playing today anyway? Are they any good?"

I laughed with him — he meant no harm — and I told him the name of the opposition and said, "I don't know how good they are."

We lost the game and I am sure that we would have lost whether or not Luigi had said anything. But I couldn't help thinking we lost, as it were, more than usual. By the final whistle we had lost the game four to one. For the whole game I watched, trying to determine whether or not Luigi had influenced the players. I was thinking that maybe Luigi had the right idea. Say something to psyche the guys, put them on their toes . . .

This was the first game that I had watched with what could be called a clinical approach. The reason for this was that after watching Michael go to pieces at a game but show talent at training, I began to think there might be more to the game than I had thought. A flickering candle at the end of a very long tunnel. If one could make a team lose by saying the wrong thing — would the opposite be possible? Luigi said what he did trying to "psyche" the team.

Did it work? To my own satisfaction I drew a conclusion. I decided that our team played worse than usual, not better. The other team had been quite mediocre, I thought. Certainly no better than our team. I was sure I had noticed a negative effect. Our players seemed to be holding back. *I decided never to tell the players that they faced a tough game and would therefore need to try very hard.*

My hunch was that it might well be best to say nothing that was negative. But it was only a hunch. I realised that if I told the team that the opposition were hopeless when they turned out to be brilliant, my credibility would be zero. If we were beaten by a hopeless team then our self-esteem would be zero! And if we did beat a hopeless team then there was not much to be proud of. But something had happened. Something negative. And I guess that was better than nothing. Maybe I had found out how to make a team lose!

Game 20

GOODBYE SECOND TEAM: GALA DAY NUMBER ONE

The last game of the season was a gala picnic day. All the parents were there with picnic lunches, having a lovely day watching soccer in the sun. The season was over. It was a beautiful sunny day, spring would soon be in the air.

We lost.

When the guys prepared to go home after the picnic I looked at them and felt I'd let them down. I felt bad, embarrassed. I felt as though I'd been wasting their time. I couldn't bring myself to say goodbye to them because all I'd been able to give them were relentless losses. They had played an entire season of soccer and not won a single game.

I was relieved it was all over, and that night I went out and got drunk. I felt very sorry for myself. I knew that a lot of the kids didn't mind half so much as I did. I knew a lot of them had been having fun — they'd been playing soccer. Winning isn't everything. (It wouldn't want to be!)

I knew that some of the rationalisations we'd been through over 20 games were more or less true. You're playing soccer for so many minutes this way and so many minutes that way, and occasionally a goal is scored. Goal scoring only takes up a minute or two — sometimes only a second or two — and you can have an enjoyable game when you lose. Some of that rationalisation was true and a lot of the kids I knew felt it that way.

After the gala day I was so depressed I couldn't talk about it to anybody. I told no one that we had not won a single game. If I hadn't discovered how to win at soccer, I'd never have told anyone. Not my mother, not my wife. Nobody. It would have died with me as a secret. I'm sure most of the players wouldn't have told anybody either.

I had a year free of soccer, and while my son played and enjoyed himself, I didn't go anywhere near it. I think his team won once or twice in the season, but I was not really interested. I thought of myself as the guaranteed World's Worst Soccer Coach. There couldn't be any competition for the title. I had had an entire season without a single win.

Game 21
HELLO THIRD TEAM

It was two years later. Summer was turning into autumn. The sun was setting earlier and a slight chill was in the air. I was having dinner with Harry Radds, my soccer playing friend, when he said, "John, we're very short of coaches." My eyes went wide. "The soccer season is just beginning and . . ."

I interrupted. "Uh, oh, forget it, Harry. No thank you, I'm rotten at coaching." I didn't tell him I had never, ever won. I was too embarrassed to go into my record too deeply.

He kept at me, and his wife kept at me. Over a few days he asked me five times. After a week or two, they were saying things like, "We're still short of coaches. The kids just want to kick the soccer ball around. You don't need to teach them anything. You don't need to be anything like a big deal and have a team and win us the cup or anything. You just have to supervise these kids enjoying themselves kicking the ball around."

I had to explain myself to them. "Look, I'm the world's worst soccer coach. I've never, ever, ever had a team that's won a game. Not ever. Not once."

They were silent. The truth was out. Public. Humiliating, but not a secret any longer. At first I realised they didn't believe me. Then, without anything being said, they realised I would not make up something like that. "Never?" said Harry, and then wished he had kept quiet.

I said, "You don't know what it's like. All I have ever done is let the boys down. I don't know the first thing about coaching. After something like six months at it I don't have the faintest idea about the game at all! And it has got to be *me*. After all I have had two teams. I have coached *two* teams right into the ground. Neither of them ever won a game with me as the coach."

They looked at each other and we changed the subject. But then a little while later Harry said, "Look, it doesn't matter whether you win or lose. It's a game. It's not life or death. What counts is playing the game—isn't it?"

I fought back, "I've heard all that before. But all I can teach them is how to lose."

He said, "Well, OK, I guess. Look, how about just looking after the boys until we can get a coach to replace you?"

I felt a real sucker as I put on my track suit two weeks later and went to the field and got a brand new team of boys. They were a different group, and this time my son Jim was included. I knew a few of the games to play in training, a few of the techniques and how to kick the ball. I bought and read more books on the subject of how to play soccer. Secretly. I hid the books from view at home in case anyone thought I might know something about the game.

Why was I doing it? Why, why, why? For Jim? No. He had been happier all last year without me. I didn't know. Maybe deep down in my consciousness I didn't want to be the worst coach in the world. Ever. In the history of the universe. Bar none. The reason was something like that.

Our first game was at our home ground on the Saturday. I looked at the team. I had written their names down and got out my list. It read, Ahab, Bob, Bennie, Charles, Ken, Edgar, Eric, Freddy, John, Jim, Dylan, Michael, Oscar, Sean. Fourteen players. I looked at them, but in my uptight state of mind I only recognised two or three of them from the training night. (And that was after spending a couple of hours with them.) I thought, "I can never remember names or faces." I said, "Well, it's only a game you guys. Concentrate on passing the ball to each other and—of course—kicking the ball into the net!"

That brought a flicker of a smile to a couple of faces. I felt slightly depressed. To exercise some authority I got out my list. I said, "Ahab goalie. Bob, Bennie and Charles are the back line. Ken, Edgar and Eric the midfield, and Freddy, John and Jim the front line."

Voices were raised. They were all talking at once. It seemed three of the guys I had called out were not even there. But we had a full team. Ahab said he had never played goalie. Sean said he was a striker. For a couple of awful minutes I changed them around, forgetting names, calling players by wrong names, going from a team of all strikers to a team of all full-backs, to a total impasse.

Finally they sorted themselves out and it was time to run onto the field. I wondered what on earth my function was. They were better off without me. I wondered how they would play. I watched. They lost the game three to nil. Afterwards I tried not to think about it. I tried to think it was their own stupid fault. They were so smart. They were the ones who lost the game, not me.

Driving home I thought, Harry will phone and ask me how we went. How did we go? We lost of course, how did he think we went. Ah, well, it *is* only a game. It's not like real life.

Game 22

SAME PROBLEMS AS
TEAMS ONE AND TWO

I spent my time trying not to think of soccer. At training I realised that the guys could all detect that I knew absolutely nothing about the game. That, I suppose, was the worst part. They all knew I was quite hopeless. I knew it too. We lost game 22.

Game 23

NOT INTERESTED

I passed through the experience of losing game 23 like an automaton. I went to training, I went to the game, I tried to think about other things. I probably wore a slightly glazed look most of the time. I felt a little like I had in schooldays occasionally — on the verge of tears but holding back. It was awful.

Game 24

THE OPPOSITION LOOK FIT

A "home" game and the visiting team looked pretty neat in green uniforms. They were gathered around one of the goals practising kicking into the net.

I said to our group, "Over here everyone." They gathered around. I said, "We are playing that green lot over there." They all looked over at the opposition. I went on, "Now they look pretty fit but I'll tell you something — *you lot look fitter*!"

I thought about when Luigi had told them the other team would be hard to beat, so play harder. And the thrashing we had taken as a result of it. So I thought I would try another line. Not giving them nonsense such as the other team are hopeless, but something different.

"You have been practising well. Kicking goals on training night was first class. Think about what we did with passing the ball. Think positively. Cooperate with each other. There is a slight wind. If we start off playing with the wind, don't forget to kick the ball high in the air and let the wind carry it. If we start off playing into the wind then keep the ball low. Now, passing the ball when you are defending . . ."

I talked for about ten minutes. All good stuff. It was not until a couple of months later that I found out something vital. Not one player had heard a *single word* I had said after "Now they look pretty fit but . . .", which was how I had started. I was to discover that if I started talking with some fact of superiority about the opposition then a shell of anxiety formed around everyone's brain that shut off further useful hearing. Careful observation would have revealed a glazed look. I did not notice it though.

I did not know it at the time, but the whole team was

thinking, "They look like a tough team." And, "Gee, this is boring." And, "I wonder how long John is going to be lecturing to us." And, "I wonder if Mum will let us eat McDonalds for lunch." And, "I'm getting sick of standing up listening to all this talking, I'll sit down. Much more comfortable." And, "I wonder if Dad knows I haven't done my homework . . ." I was talking to myself, and myself alone.

We lost two to nil.

Game 25

THE WIND AND THE SUN

I had often heard parents, spectators and players talking about playing against the wind and playing into the sun. Their talk, without exception, was negative. They only talked about the bad effects of nature on their own team. I did a bit of homework and even wrote down a few notes. Basically, if the wind was against you it could only be for half the game, then it would be behind you. So why worry? The same with the sun. If it was in your eyes one way it was in your opponents' eyes the other half. It all seemed quite simple and also fair. But still I heard people talking about it in a negative way. I realised that if it was possible to think about it negatively then the opposite might also be possible. During the week I had made the following notes:

The wind
If it is against you, blowing in your face as you attack:
When you are dribbling the wind will hold the ball close to your feet as you run, the ball will not get away from you easily, you can run very fast. Like kicking a ball uphill; always kick the ball low when you are kicking into the wind, keeping it near to the ground where the wind will not affect it too much.
If the wind is behind you:
Kicking the ball high in the air will carry it with the wind down the field. Get your toe underneath the ball for the appropriate kick; when dribbling with the ball you only have to tap it very lightly to keep it ahead of you; find a gentle slope for players to practice on both uphill and downhill.

The sun
If you are attacking with the sun behind you then balls that you lob at the opponents' goal from the sunny sky will be hard for them to see. (This was a ploy used by the Royal Air Force in World War II.)

I was quite pleased with my concepts. I talked to the team about them before the game and received quite a reasonable response. They appeared to be listening to me. They liked the ideas and even tried them, once or twice quite obviously, and we scored a goal with a beautiful lob.

We lost the game, but maybe I was headed in the right direction. Positive thinking. Work out the mechanics and the physics of the thing — perhaps that was the clue.

Game 26
CHANGED POSITIONS AT TRAINING

At training the guys seemed more receptive. I told everybody to play in different positions to the last game and we would have a game with one of the other teams on the training field. The coach of the other team said he would referee the game.

I placed Bob, whose mother drove him to games in a Mercedes sports, in the front row. He had always been a full back. Bingo. After about ten minutes he scored a goal. I shouted out congratulations. I ran over to the Mercedes. Bob's two younger brothers were sitting in the car. I said, "Your brother just scored a goal!" The effect on Bob of scoring the goal was marvellous. His game improved out of sight. I spoke to his mother later and she said that the previous week Bob had been talking about giving up soccer. The single goal changed his mind. And then she said, "Thank you very much, John, for telling his brothers. That was just about as important as actually scoring the goal. He is their hero now."

In game 26 he did it. He scored a goal in a real game. We did not win the game, but I had my first insight that there were things involved beyond the obvious. I think that is when the dreaded word "psychology" may have crossed my mind. I had a feeling when I was telling his brothers that I was not just spreading the joy. Making him a hero to his own brothers would surely lift his self-esteem and that must be good for him.

The possibility impinged on my mind that perhaps the whole situation was not all unadulterated gloom and despair. I felt certain I had turned Bob into one of life's heroes, rather than one of its victims. Well, soccer-wise at least.

Even though we lost the game there was a certain feeling in the air. I felt I had done something managerial—changing their positions on the field—and something had happened; Bob had scored a goal. Maybe there was hope.

Game 27

THINK WIN

I had heard the expression "Think Win" as being one way of thinking oneself into winning something. A kind of bad grammar style of positive thinking. Dale Carnegie and all that. Or rather what I thought Dale Carnegie was all about at the time. (I have since read his books and changed my mind about what he was advocating.) So although I had read practically nothing about the "Think Win" style of coaching, I lectured the team on how to Think Win. Something must have been "in the air" because as I spoke they did not get that terrible glazed look. I spoke for about five to ten minutes and they seemed to listen all the time. They raced onto the field for the game with more than their usual enthusiasm.

At half-time we were two goals down. But we had played quite well. So at the half-time break I gave them some more "Think Win" talk. I know now what I did not know then. They tried harder. They kicked harder. They ran faster. They secreted large quantities of adrenalin into their bodies. Their style of play took on a desperate appearance, although I did not realise it at the time. I thought they were trying harder and I thought that was what was required to win the game.

We lost five to one. I didn't know what to think at the time. "Think Win" had done something. But we had lost. Maybe I was nearly on the right track, I thought. Now I know I was nowhere near the mark. Now, when I see a game where the losing team runs faster, kicks harder, tries harder, in fact does everything in the way of expending more energy, I know their kicks are going to go wide of the mark. And the more they lose the angrier they will get. And the harder they will try.

If only I had known it at the time, the real slogan I should have used was "Know How to Win". It is not just difficult to "Think Win" when you are losing, it is practically impossible. It is a contradiction in terms. How can you think about winning when you are losing? Maybe you can before the game, but to try it when you are down two goals seems silly. Now. It didn't at the time, though.

Game 28

NEVER CRITICISE

At training I thought about using the management techniques of Winning Friends and Influencing People. One of the tenets I had heard was Never Criticise.

I tried it. I realised that I had been quite critical. Especially when the team lost. (Which was all the time!) So I resolved to never criticise a player and restrict my comments to praise only. Whenever a player made a good move I lavished praise on him. Whenever a player made a foolish move I said either nothing or perhaps, "Better luck next time." It seemed to lift their spirits, or so I thought. Maybe I was just hoping it would.

We lost anyway. But I could not see any bad effects from not criticising players at all, so I thought I would stay with it — no criticism, ever. I thought of ways around it. If a player was half-asleep and let the ball go past him I would go over the incident afterwards, and instead of criticising him I would say, "Now, Dylan, when you kick the ball a long way, try to stay *wide awake* and *alert* so that you will be able to stop the ball if it comes back to you."

Game 29

THE ODDS AGAINST WINNING ARE NOW 29 TO 1

I worked out that I had coached 28 games. The thought was a bit mind-boggling. The twenty-ninth game was the real low point.

We lost the game. I stared at the players like a zombie as they ran about the field. I felt nothing. I did not know it at the time, but it was the lowest point from many aspects. I did not care whether they won or lost. It was just a stupid game, kicking about a piece of some poor animal's hide blown up with air. Who cared? Not me. Maybe I cared for the poor animal. As I drove home from the game I still felt nothing. I thought maybe I can put up with this until the end of the season and then quit for good. I supposed it was not too much hassle. Just kicking a ball about. Soccer was a really boring game.

Game 30

RESPONSIBILITY FELLS AHAB

My thirtieth game. The most important game I have ever watched in my life. A game I will never forget. There was a light at the end of the tunnel, it was not just an illusion. I sighted it very briefly in this game. It took less than one second, and then it was gone. Thank goodness I was watching.

The game took place at a ground a few kilometres away. The opposition was a good team but we were not making it too easy for them. Most of the action was taking place around our goal and we were defending more or less the whole time. No one had scored but the opposition had nearly scored about five times. Good luck and good defence by our backs had kept the ball out of our net. And then it happened.

Every player except their goalie was in our half of the field. Ahab, one of our best players, got the ball. He was the fastest runner in our team and also probably faster than any player in the opposition team. He was right near the middle of the field and there wasn't another player near him. He took the ball and he kicked it in the right direction, and he ran and he ran as fast as his little legs would take him. Like a cheetah. Every few strides he would lightly touch the ball, keeping it just in front of him. The nearest player to him was ten or fifteen paces behind him and falling further behind with each step. Here was a certain goal coming up and I jumped for joy on the sidelines.

I cheered him at the top of my voice and so did every spectator from our side, his father loudest of all. Ahab ran like the wind and there was nobody who could catch him. He had the ball and he kept it in front of him, just gave it light little taps. I could see our opponents' goalie standing transfixed with fright. Their goalie couldn't move, he couldn't think of what to do because this guy was running straight at him and any second the ball was going to fly past him and into the net. How could one player stop the goal, the goal area felt so large behind him. And then, as I watched, Ahab tripped and fell. The ball rolled slowly down into their goalie's hands and the crowd went ooooohh!

I turned away from the field and I held my head in my hands. What on earth had tripped him up? He was a brilliant runner. He usually fell over less than any player on the team. I cursed the rotten field. What an outrage, expecting players to play on a field so rough that ordinary running was just impossible. Anger started to well up within me. I walked a few paces away from the game. I was in deep shock but I wasn't sure why. Adrenalin was pumping through my system. I watched the rest of the game — we lost one goal to nil — in a trance.

When the final whistle blew I walked across the field. I walked over to the patch of ground where Ahab had fallen. I was looking for a rut, a ridge, some uneven turf. Horrified I looked down. It was as smooth as a putting green on a golf course. What had tripped him? Even as the question presented itself — what could trip someone on a perfectly smooth field — the realisation began to creep into my brain. I had tripped him. I must have tripped him as surely as Ken's father had tripped Ken that day long ago. I put two and two together. I realised why Ahab had fallen. For 30 games in a row I had been making my team lose. I had made Ahab fall over as certainly as if I'd pushed him. As certainly as Ken's father had brought Ken down to the ground by shouting at him.

But how? That was the question. How? I knew I was the one who had done it, but how had I done it? And how could I find out? I was in no doubt. I had tripped Ahab from a distance of 50 metres! His brain had sent fast running signals to his legs until that last moment. Then the signals had gone wrong. One leg had hit the other and down he went. And the certain goal was a goal no more.

What was involved? Over the next few days I started to

find out. Ahab apparently felt all the people around the side of the field as well as all his team-mates were relying on him, and trusting him with that goal. The responsibility fogged his brain and sent the signals to his legs that tripped him. Actually, I suppose his inner thigh muscles contracted slightly more than they should have and one foot, coming forward, brushed against the foot that was on the ground, and crash.

He couldn't carry the responsibility. That wasn't quite the word but it seemed near the mark. Maybe it was like a force, I thought, the feeling of people depending on him, which brought him down to the ground. Some force. An invisible force that could knock someone down. And if there was such a force, the ramifications seemed immense. Could I find out what it was?

I went home and found an armchair and sat in it and stared at the wall. I had a silent talk with myself. "John, you've been transmitting to your players something that makes them lose. You mightn't be able to put in into words. It might be just a feeling or something. Whether or not you can put it into words it's quite certain that they're not losing every week because they are bad players."

That was the bombshell that hit my consciousness. Their losses were not totally a function of their ability at the game. Something had been making them lose. Something had been making the two previous teams I coached lose. Three teams. The common factor? Me. Three teams had lost 30 games. They had lost to good teams and bad teams. That was the part that made me think. They were not handicapped in any way and there wasn't any real football reason or athletic reason or physical reason for them to always lose. So a psychological reason seemed to be a fair bet. It's logical that if you have some good players they are going to score the odd goal. Some of the teams we played were hopeless. But we lost to them. Here we had a certain goal and still lost. "Face the facts, John, in some way you have been transmitting a losing syndrome into your player's minds."

If that were so, would it be possible for the World's Worst Soccer Coach to reverse the situation? Certainly no other soccer coach in history could have coached three different teams to 30 games and lost every one of them. Could the World's Worst Soccer Coach transmit the Winning Syndrome? If I could transmit a losing force, could the opposite be possible? My skin went slightly goose fleshed as I considered it. Did the logic follow that whatever it was that I gave them to make them lose, could I give them something to make them win? I sat for a long time thinking about it. After about an hour I came to the conclusion that I had better try to find out.

What could I lose apart from the next game? It seemed worth a try. I thought perhaps it had nothing much to do with soccer. However, if I were a brilliant soccer player then the players would certainly listen to me. But the more I thought about it, the more I thought I was probably headed in the wrong direction. The answer should not have required me to become a famous soccer player. Although I might have needed a champion player to coach the team, I was certain there was more involved. I sat down with a pencil and paper and wrote down a few of these things.

I analysed the time Ken's father brought him down. I thought if a brilliant soccer player — a hero soccer player who played for his country — could coach my lads he may be able to enthuse them. If that were possible, I felt a responsibility. I would shift from my job as coach and call myself manager. I'd manage the team because somebody had to look after all the gear, and I would employ guest soccer players, brilliant soccer players, to coach the kids and teach them to win. That was one option and I wrote it down. I knew where I could contact champion players and maybe have guest appearances and so on. It was a dismal weekend, but it finished with a little hope.

On Monday morning I went to work. I felt a little like the skinny guy in the Charles Atlas advertisement who had sand kicked in his face by the big bully and then decided to take the Charles Atlas muscle-building course and go and teach that bully a lesson he'd never forget. I must find out where they teach the lessons.

It was a nice day that Monday. At lunchtime I walked

through a bookshop in the city and stopped in the section marked Applied Psychology and looked over the titles. I did not even look for the section marked Sports. I picked up a book and leafed through it. I looked through several books. I looked at their tables of contents. I bought one and that night I read some of it.

The next day I bought another book similar to the first one. I discovered that a lot of bookstores had sections on applied psychology. Some called it one thing, some another. Some mixed it in with the business section, some in the health section. It seemed a weird and wonderful genre. The books were all about how to improve yourself, how to live better, how to live without worry, how to make friends, how to win friends and influence people. The list of books that I bought was quite a long one. (See bibliography for the final list.)

Now there is an obvious piece of nonsense that needs an answer here and now. What if everybody read this book? How can both teams win a game of soccer? Naturally they cannot.

Firstly, not everyone will buy this book. Secondly, many who read this book will be looking for a trick. They will look for one concise little sentence that sums it all up. They will try to precis and condense the system into a shortened form. Nothing I can say will inhibit them. Whether they fail or not is up to them — I wish them luck. And they will look for a formula like a chemical formula. Alas, when one is dealing with a team of human beings, formulas need constant monitoring and altering. There is no one meaningful phrase to describe it all. Most will miss the point because if there was a single thought that could win games, you would not be reading a book about it. In fact the situation is even worse than that. If there is a small trace element in the Team System in this book it is possible that it is like arsenic. It may well work perfectly and not poison anybody as long as it is carried by the bulk of the rest of the ingredients. But it is poisonous by itself.

The system described in this book should not be shortened. I am sure that bits taken out of context could be misinterpreted. I imagine the Team System could be used for something besides soccer. But one element of the system out of context or in a different semantic environment will often be just nonsense.

I commenced to read the applied psychology books with fervour. Every night. I took some to work and became a little embarrassed at their titles. So I covered several of the books with brown paper.

BOOK II
GAMES 31 TO 60

Game 31

NO ROUGH STUFF PLEASE

It was Friday night before the match. I was very excited. I put off going to bed because my mind was in a whirl. I was trying to think of all I had read all at once. What was I on to? How should I handle it? I had discovered something. Or had I? The overwhelming factor seemed to be that the players felt — well, what did they feel? Anxiety? Responsibility? And did all players feel that way (whatever way it was), or was it just Ahab? The questions all seemed rhetorical! Ahab was a tough guy. He had brothers, older brothers. And he was about as far from being a sissy as it was possible to be. He was a "boy" in the Arab sense and quite different from their cultural "girl". So what on earth was he afraid of? And if he was afraid, then surely all the other players were afraid more than he was. Was he scared of getting his shins kicked? Never.

I sat in my favourite chair and closed my eyes. I tried to imagine myself in his place as he was running up the field and about to score. I tried to hear the crowd cheering "me" on. I tried to dream. There I was. The ball at my feet. Past the halfway mark and no opposition. Nothing but the goalie to beat. No other player near me. I was going fast. I was touching the ball about every three or four paces, sometimes with my left foot, sometimes with my right. No problems. I was careful not to kick it too hard and out of my reach. Go, go, go. Just a light tap every few paces. I was confident no player could catch me. I forgot about my pursuers as they fell further behind. I was in complete control. I looked up at the goal every few paces. Wouldn't my father be pleased! Three-quarters of the way up the field. I was running fast but easily.

The crowd was shouting, everybody on the sidelines was

shouting. My father would be shouting loudly. Come on . . .
The cheering, the shouting. Go, go, go. They were all shouting
at me. Everyone's attention was on *me*. I was going to score
the goal that would win the game. It was all up to me. Me.
I looked down at the ball as I ran. My God, I thought, what
if I failed?

That was it! That *had* to be it. I got up from my chair
and walked around the room. It was a crushing feeling of
responsibility. Or something like it. It was some kind of fear
of failure. And it had made Ahab trip himself. On smooth
ground his muscles had made one foot brush against the other
as he ran and down he had fallen. By midnight I had decided
to tell the team that the responsibility for winning or losing
was mine, not theirs. They would then be "free" to win. I
probably had a smile on my face that night as I slept.

Saturday dawned. The game. Game 31. I ate breakfast
and thought about how I would say it. And the more I thought
the more silly it sounded. How could I assume responsibility
when we had never won a game? Could I blame tactics? Give
them a new game plan — it would not matter exactly what it
was, after all, as long as it was mine and I could say that the
old plans had failed.

As I picked up the gear and a few players I formalised
what I would say to them. We arrived at the field. I watched
our players kicking the ball around, "warming up". They
seemed happy enough. Pleased to see each other, friends
playing ball together. And in a moment I completely changed
my mind. I think I sensed them looking at the opposition team.
I looked over at the other team. They were at the same stage
of preparation as us. Some had their playing tops on, some
did not. Their coach was talking to a couple of them . . .

A brainwave hit me. I formalised it. I thought, our team
look as though they are apprehensive about getting their shins
kicked, not about the weight of responsibility. You have been
fooling yourself, John. I called out, "Over here everybody."
My mind was going at full speed. I called to a couple of players
who had not heard me and they all assembled around. Some
who had not changed, changed their tops for team tops.

"Quiet," I said. "Now listen. Today I want no rough stuff!"

Their eyes seemed to open wide. The hair on the back of my head actually crawled! Their eyes had not glazed over!

"The other team are only young kids and I want none of their mothers saying we smashed their little sons about."

Our team looked across at the opposition and back at me and *their eyes had still not glazed over!* "You, you and you are the back line. You are goalie for the first half and you swap with Eric at half-time. Don't argue. I'm in charge here. You are just playing a game and having a good time. If you don't win then it's my fault, not yours."

They looked excited. I had not seen the look before. They seemed taller! I reiterated their playing positions: four in the front row, three centre and three backs, goalie. "This looks like an easy game. Have fun."

I thought about saying No Kicking of Shins as a final call but time slipped away from me and they were gone, onto the field. What the hell, I thought. Who am I kidding? Who do you think you are, John, and what do you think you are doing? I'll tell you who you are. You are the World's Worst Coach, that's who. But the seed of a thought came to me. Why not experiment with what you say? Seeing that you always lose the game anyway. Why not try all different things? You could even write them down. Record what you tell the team and what effect it had. Yes, I could do that. (And of course I did!) But as I dreamed on in an academic fog of applied psychology I was electrified by the action on the field.

Our team had the ball at the opposition's end of the field and we had four or five players attacking! And they had been playing for only about ten minutes. I heard them call to each other twice. I had never seen them playing like it. The ball went into the net and I screamed. "Fantastic," I cried. "You beauty . . ."

All our mothers and fathers were shouting. Everyone from our side of the contest was smiling. I kept shouting praise at them as they ran back to the centre of the field for the post-goal kick-off. They were all smiling. It had worked. (I stopped shouting just short of embarrassing them.) They had been frightened. And they had overcome their fear. The miracle had come to pass.

I knew that if I had said, "Don't be frightened" I would have got the old glazed look in response. I knew – I had read as much – that if you tell someone "Don't be frightened" the most likely word that they hear is "frightened" and that is all they hear. If I had said "Don't do this" or "Do that" in the normal way, all they would have heard in that atmosphere before the game would have been the "this or that" and they would not have heard the "do" or the "don't". So, from the books I had read that week I came up with the new angle. Telling them not to be rough was in retrospect almost laughable considering they were frightened about getting their shins kicked! But it seemed to make them think, "We don't need to kick shins to win this game. We will go easy on this other team who are afraid of us kicking their shins." And as they thought (what I really mean is that I thought they thought) about how they were not going to give the other team a hard time they seemed to stand taller. It was as though they did not *need* to kick shins.

The half-time whistle blew with the score at our one goal to their nil. We were winning. For the first time in my soccer history, we were winning. It was smiles into our oranges. I had one as well. Not much talking, and talk was all happy. No freaky talk about anything hard or tough or bad, only happy talk. No "coach" talk, only praise from me. Lavish praise. Not one word of criticism, I knew that much from the week's reading. I patted several of them on the back. (I felt like hugging them.)

The other team was on the field and I quickly organised a slight reshuffle of positions – goalie swapped with a full-back and so on – and they ran onto the field for the second half. There had been no noticeable wind or other condition that needed talking about.

Second half. Both teams came near to scoring once or twice each but no goals. The final whistle blew. One-nil. We had won!

I ran onto the field and shouted three cheers for the other

team. Our team gave three rousing cheers. Louder than ever before. I told them how fantastic they were. I kept telling them. I remembered what I had read. Lavish praise. Unrestricted. I shook every player by the hand as we all walked off. Some I had to grab for their hands, some stuck theirs out. Everybody smiling. Parents, friends, players, and most of all the coach.

Then I noticed something. I didn't pay much attention to it at the time, but I noticed it. Two or three of the parents were not smiling. I bulldozed in. I said, "Weren't they *fantastic?*" and forced a positive response out of them. I named their child and said, "Didn't Freddie (or whoever) play brilliantly?" so that the player could hear the parent's response.

I thought, "I can *win!*" I didn't even blush. I didn't think about the "I" until a little later. Now, much later, now I can blush. Because I hadn't won anything. What I had done was clear the way so the players could play their best. Maybe it could be called "psyching" but it was not the kind of psyching I had heard about. Nor was it like anything I had tried before. I had seen rugby players on TV slapping each other's faces before a game to stir themselves up. I guess to make them fighting mad. Well, my psyching was nothing like that at all. I began to think of what I was doing as psychotherapy. Maybe I was making the players enthusiastic. Or something . . .

I collected the gear and two players and my son Jim to drive home in my car. Our entire conversation was about what a great game it had been. I thought, "I can conquer the world!"

I dropped off two ecstatic players who ran into their homes shouting out the good news. I thought, "John, you have unlocked the secrets of the universe."

I dropped Jim off at a friend's place to play, so I arrived at home alone. My wife did not know we had never won, ever. She knew we usually lost, though. I said to her, "Well, we won today, darling."

She said, "Oh, great, darling. I'm happy for you. Was it a good game?"

"Yes, good fun. They played well." I found a lounge chair and sat quietly in it. I thought about my father. He used to tell me things like, "John, it's not the ball that Life bowls you that counts. It's how you play the game." (He was captain of his school cricket team.) I thought, who would have bet on my team to win this morning? Answer — only a crazy person. What were the odds? We were a team that had played together for about ten games and had never ever won one. Ten to one against? No; more likely about a thousand to one against. We had beaten the odds. We had brought home a thousand to one shot and it had not been an accident. It had been deliberate. We had turned the world around. Life had dealt us a hand of nothing in particular. Not a single ace. But we had played and won.

I sat and hugged myself. I could hardly contain my joy. When Liverpool or maybe Tottenham Hotspurs heard about me — well I may as well stand by the letterbox and wait for the offers. I could imagine the TV cameras zooming in on me sitting next to Brian Clough, the famous manager, up north watching Nottingham Forest play. Jim came home for dinner and of course was thrilled to bits at his first win. Our joy lasted seven days.

Game 32

TOO SMUG: BACK TO THE BOOKS

Game 32 came along. Saturday morning. I had not read a single book all week. Everyone was smiling as we met at the game. The players kicked a few balls around as a "warm-up" and put their tops on one by one. Time for the game drew near and I gathered them around and gave them playing positions. I thought about labouring the point of the previous week and how to say it without "giving away the secret" and without them thinking they had been tricked in some way.

I said a bit about them being winners and not having to play rough. I drew a neat line between telling them they did not need to play rough without overdoing it. The feedback seemed good. No player seemed apprehensive. I was more than pleased with my talk. It was not too much of one thing or another. I was friendly, praising them, trying to give them confidence.

They ran onto the field, the whistle blew and away they went. They played well. At half-time there was no score at all. Nil–all. A good game. Back to the game with changed ends. And then disaster struck.

The opposition scored a goal. I became tense. I became worried. As the end of the game drew near I was having to cheer myself up with things like, "Never mind, John, whatever happens you are not a born loser. And neither are your players. And that is the main thing. It's just a game."

The final whistle blew. We had lost one to nil.

As I ran onto the field and shouted three cheers for the other team my depression lifted a little. I said to the opposition Coach, "Thanks for a good game."

He said, "Yes, they were quite evenly matched. It was a

good game." He shook my hand as we said goodbye.

I looked up at the sky. It was overcast and the wind was cold. I thought, "John, if you can do it once you can do it again." I hadn't found the key to the universe at all. But I was not frowning, I was smiling. I was sure I was headed in the right direction. What was needed was more study.

On Sunday I read some more. I could hardly wait for Monday to come around, because I had a plan. Not for the team — for myself. Monday meant the bookshops were open! More books! I bought two more books on Monday and on Tuesday I cruised around the bookshops. I bought three more even though I had not read even one of the two I had bought on Monday. My plan, in retrospect, seemed to be that the more books I bought the better we would be.

I was right, but not because of sheer numbers. The reason was that some small pieces in some books electrified my thinking. But large sections of many of the books were almost boring. Not boring in their content, but trite and obvious. Like tell the group not to be frightened. Well, I knew that to be nonsense. To tell someone not to be frightened does not usually make them less frightened. A lot of the information in the books just did not apply to my situation. I wondered if it was the same for everybody. I wondered if some bits of some books made good sense to some people and other bits made sense to other people.

I could read several chapters and then one sentence would flash at me. Yes, I would think. That's how it is! But that was all. Just the one sentence. And the rest of the book might be meaningless to me. And yet in the winning game (*the* winning game, I thought, the one and only winning game) the thought had worked for everyone on the team. Really, just one little sentence. But the right one at the right time and place. Puzzling. But I read voraciously.

I had studied speed reading and I read at about 500 words per minute with 85 per cent comprehension. (Not particularly brilliant. My wife did the same course and topped 1,000 words per minute with over 90 per cent comprehension.) But as I read, as fast as I could, the same thing kept happening. I would read page after page, fast, and then suddenly I would stop. I would stare at a sentence, or paragraph. My mind would run. That's how things really are, I would think. Mmm . . . Then read on as fast as I could.

There was obviously much more to the whole concept of playing a game than just being frightened. I read the phrase the Fear of Failure. I liked it.

By the end of the week I had several concepts: fear of getting your shins kicked; fear of everybody depending on me (I had not discarded that one); unknown.

I knew instinctively that there was more to it than I had put together so far. But what? Maybe it was not fear at all but something completely different. Maybe anxiety . . .

The game is analogous to life in one respect: the game is played for 90 minutes. A goal can be scored in a minute or even a few seconds. The team can be in a losing position, defending its goal desperately, then get the ball away from its goal and up the field and into the opponents' goal in a minute or two. The record may be just ten or 20 seconds. Some team games have huge scores. Basketball games often finish with scores like 100 to 90. Most soccer scores are just a goal or two for a whole game. Many soccer games are drawn with no score at all. Many are won with a score of one to nil.

Life can be looked at like that, I thought. You play the game, and you either enjoy it or not as your disposition dictates, and then for a short burst your opportunity arrives and requires intense concentration. You score the goal and resume your normal lifestyle.

You play soccer running, kicking, heading the ball, carefully passing it to your team-mates, and then — in a split second — the opportunity. You might find yourself in front of the opponents' goal, ten paces out, and the ball comes in from the side. You have to kick it at right angles to the line of flight to kick it into the net. You have to judge its speed and trajectory and it must bounce off your foot and into the goal. The angle of incidence must be exact. That split second can win or lose the game. It can win or lose the championship. It could mean a million dollars one way or the other, whether it goes into the net or not.

Put yourself in the position of the player for a moment. There you are, moving towards the opponents' goal, you know where all the nearby players are, where the goal and the goalkeeper are and you work out the angle that you will need to kick the ball so it will score a goal. And you work everything out in a very short time. Right then, with a split second to go before the kick, a still small voice within your head says, "Don't forget that everyone is depending on you. A million dollars is riding on this kick, thousands of fans are watching you, so whatever you do, *don't fail*!"

What happens? Signals come from your brain down to your leg as it swings forward and bang, you kick the ball so hard it goes right over the top of the net and into the spectators. Or you trip. Or worst of all, you miss the ball altogether.

If you are worrying about something you will possibly miss the ball. If you are thinking that the coach is watching you, it is possible to kick at fresh air. For total concentration has a precondition. It is this. Nothing — but nothing — must be overlayed around your brain that will inhibit your concentration. You must not even think anything like "This goal will win the game!". You must only be thinking about getting the ball into the net. Not about what it means. Not about the consequences of a miss or a score.

If one of your players is in a better position to score, your concentration level must allow you to pass the ball to your team-mate without thinking any thoughts about personality, about self, about anything, except — getting the ball into the net. You pass the ball to your team-mate and you do it so that the ball is in the best position for him to kick it. This is the essence of belonging to a team. The objective of the team has a higher priority than anything personal.

Incredible as it may seem, emotions like jealousy can produce a pass that is a fraction out of reach for your team-mate, or a little too near him so that he has to slow down slightly. There is an analogy with a number of drugs. A fogging effect seems to invade the brain from any of: anxiety, fear of failure, heroin, alcohol, marijuana, jealousy, hate, anger, responsibility, worry and so on. Maximum concentration requires that all these mental situations be minimised.

And of course smugness is just about the opposite of concentration. That Saturday afternoon I rated smugness as another of the Deadly Sins, like sloth. Back to the books with — yes — concentration.

I was up to my ears in theory. I could hardly wait for the weekend to come around to test the theory. Gone was the boredom. Gone the worry. Everything was excitement. Roll on the next thrilling game . . . My, how the world had turned around.

Game 33
EVERYBODY HAS TO BE FRIENDLY

I read books all week. As I read I wondered about my theory. I thought about the last game. And how we had lost it with my theory so firmly in place. I had thought of calling it the Fear of Failure Theory.

The sense of responsibility and the fear of failure had seemed to be like playing in deep sand. When the players felt free of those kinds of emotions they were able to operate in a different environment altogether and really concentrate on what they were doing. This was more than theory. I had watched their game. Their play was very noticeably improved.

For 30 games — and with different players — I had been transmitting, albeit unconsciously, some kind of performance fear. Then I had passed out the firm order — no rough stuff. The team had then played as though they had been freed from something that had been holding them back. The more I thought about it the more I became sure that they had all felt the fear (or whatever it was that they felt) ever since I first had any contact with the game.

I considered the options as I read book after book. With each book I would read as fast as I could and as soon as I found a provocative part I would stop reading and stare into space. I would try to fit each new thought into my Fear of Failure Theory. Sometimes it would fit, sometimes it would not. Sometimes an applied psychology book would tell me something that I had tried time and again but instead of success it had brought failure. As I had a 100 per cent score of losses up to game 31 I had a perfect statistical sample to work with. I knew what I had said to players. And I knew what did not inspire them. But as I read, the puzzle seemed to assume a different shape. I tried to think "academically".

Here is what I came up with that week. Perhaps the Fear of Failure Theory was OK as far as it went. But perhaps the removal of Fear of Failure was not an answer in itself. Perhaps it was just a necessary *precondition*. Yes, that seemed to make sense. Perhaps lots of the things I had been saying to the players over all the losing games had been said with the fear of failure hanging over the scene and clouding everything.

I knew that there were many ways as yet untried (by me) to remove the fear of failure. Basically I could laugh and joke before every game and convince every player that it was just that — a game — and winning or losing was incidental. I knew that if I could project a devil-may-care attitude I could lift the dreaded fears. But what then? Just a repeat of everything I had said before all those games? I knew from reading that the answer was neither yes nor no. I found out that although I may have been saying the right things I had been saying them in the wrong way or at the wrong time.

As I drove to the thirty-third game I thought over what I was going to say. I pulled into the kerb. I had two players in the car, one of them Jim. I said I was just going to buy a newspaper and I went into a newsagency. But that was not the real reason. The reason I had to move about was that I suddenly realised that I was falling victim to the dreaded Fear of Failure *myself*! I was worrying about the possibility of saying the wrong thing! I was extremely uptight and nervous.

I walked around inside the shop and stared at the magazine racks. I realised that I was looking at girlie magazines. Naked girls stretched out on a dozen different covers. I went to the cashier, bought a newspaper and got back in the car.

At the game the players gathered, put on their tops. There were parents and friends all around. I couldn't ask them to go away. So I said "OK everybody, over here"; I walked across the field and (thank goodness) the players followed me and no one else came. The Pied Piper. Adrenalin was making my fingers tingle. I called out to two stragglers and when I was well out of earshot of anyone (other than the players) I addressed them.

"We are a team. We are more than a group of players. We are a group of friends out to have a good time playing soccer."

No glazed looks.

"I have said it before, everybody in this team has to be friends *whether they like it or not*."

They had never heard anything quite like this.

"Now, everybody look at each other." A couple of players sneaked sideways looks at other players. I did not panic. And I knew that I must not go too far. I knew I was moving near to a precipice of embarrassment for them. I had already decided I would not ask for any hand-shaking or touching, just looking.

"Go on, look at each other. Look at every other member of this team. From the smallest to the largest you are all members of this one team. From the fastest to the slowest. And you have to recognise each other *instantly*! Look right around at everyone else."

Slowly they turned their heads and looked at each other, thank God without embarrassment. They just looked — slow ones and fast ones, big ones and little ones. I kept quiet for about 10 or 15 long seconds.

"Now another thing. If someone is getting on your tit, well — not here. Not allowed. You *have* to cooperate here, and being friendly and pleasant is the order of the day. And if being friendly seems too hard to do then you have to be pleasant. You have to at least *act* friendly. If anybody wants to fight, well they have to wait until after the game. Because this team has *no aggro* in it at all. None. If anybody has a grudge, forget it. While you are in this team — no fights. No arguments. Friends, whether you like it or not. By order. No exceptions. Everybody understand?"

A couple of nodding heads. It may have been subjective thinking but I think the smaller players looked happy with the new order.

"You, you and you are midfielders. You on the right, you on the left. You on the right wing on the forward line . . ." and so on with positions. "Have a good game. Let's go."

What a game. At half-time we were winning three to nil. I spent the half-time break going over what fun they were having, laughing and joking with them. No lecturing. At full-time we had a score line of four to nil. Oh, joy. And all through the game I found myself noticing the same thing. The best players were playing as they usually played. Maybe improved, maybe not. But the smallest players, the skinny little ones, the timid ones. They were something else. They played as though they had all grown bigger.

As I drove away from the game I was feeling great. I did not feel as though I had personally won the game (as I had felt with our first win). I felt as though I had found a way that *let* them win. A way that set them free and *allowed* them to play their best. In fact, better than their previous best. And most important of all—I knew that I must not relax and think I was the hottest thing on two legs. I knew I was onto something and whatever it was it didn't seem quite like it had two weeks ago. Perhaps it was not a theory I was formulating. Maybe it was more like a system.

I knew there was a lot more reading to do. And I knew that I had at long last been dealt an ace. The old ace in the hole from the game of stud poker. What was the ace? It was this: I could try something out with the players and since I was taking notes, *it didn't matter if we lost*. I had been looking at the hand Life had dealt me all the time and I had never even noticed that ace. If we did something that resulted in a loss it was just as valuable as a win. It told us *what not to do*.

I was in fact the privileged observer in an applied psychology "laboratory". And for the system or experiment to be valid there probably *should* be a couple of losses, just for balance. But I was also more than an observer. I was using the applied psychology I was learning to combat my personal fear of failure. And it had worked.

The parents and friends who had seen us win two out of the last three games (notice the propaganda of statistics!) were very happy. They had seen so many losses and they were so happy that the cycle had been broken that they were actually saying to me, "It's only a game" when we were *winning*! (Something they had not said enough when we were losing, when it might have helped.)

The scoreboard read: games won—two. Games lost—31. But the way I was feeling was more like the other way around. For the first time in a long, long time I was starting to have some fun. Some real fun.

Game 34

RECALL POSITIVE MOVES

They all had their tops on and we had about 20 minutes before the game was due to start. "Over here everybody. Sit down if you want to." Some sat down. "I have been reading about visualising." Dumb looks. "Visualising. Here is what it is. It means going over in your mind the ways you played that were great. You don't think about mistakes or anything that you did wrong at all. Only the good parts."

No glazed-over look in their eyes. Great. "Now Freddy. Remember last week when you kicked the ball and their goalie stopped it, then dropped it?"

Freddy said, "And then I put it in."

"You certainly did. Now go over that in your mind. You had tried to score, but had failed. But instead of standing back and thinking, 'Oh, hell, the goalie stopped it', you followed it in and like magic the ball bounced off the goalie and landed at your feet. And you put it straight into the back of the net like a champion."

Big smiles.

"Now think about it. Although you had made the first kick you didn't relax. You stayed right there on your toes." We all thought about it in silence for a few seconds. "Get the idea, everyone? Just the good parts."

I went on, "Freddy, you didn't give up the moment it didn't work out for you. Which would have been very easy to do. And who could have blamed you? Now think about it. Picture yourself making the first kick and keeping on your toes to see what happens. Keep going over it in your mind."

I turned to a little player. "Bennie, remember when you had about ten players around you and you shot the ball out through a gap to — who was it — Eric?"

"Yes," said little Bennie, "I saw Eric out of the corner of my eye . . ."

I said, "And you stabbed the ball out to him."

"Yes."

I thought, "I am *not* talking to some undersized kid (who is short on talent) about three seconds of meaningless play that went nowhere a week ago; I am communicating with another human being."

I said to Bennie, "Go over it in your mind. Think about how you kicked the ball. You have the ball, you see Eric, you see the gap in all those legs, you kick . . . sideways?"

Bennie said, "Yes, I kicked with the outside of my right foot, sideways."

"Great. You passed the ball when you were absolutely walled in by players."

I could see the idea was working, not just on the players I was talking about but the ones listening were getting the same buzz. Especially hearing Bennie — the smallest player in the team — talking about the game like an actual player with thoughts about the game.

Then I had a mini-crisis myself. I knew not to talk about mistakes but I didn't know if the mere mention of mistakes was death and depression and failure, or not. I decided to risk it. I said, "Don't think about your mistakes at all. As far as I am concerned, mistakes are bullshit. Nobody makes mistakes on purpose and when you make a mistake you certainly know when you make one. You don't want to go over *that* in your mind. Just the good parts. *Everybody* makes mistakes. Only think about the good bits. If you did a good kick that went exactly where you wanted it to go — think about that."

Time was running out, the other team was moving onto the field. Our team looked happy. I said, "Let's do some more visualising at training next week." At least three or four voices said yes.

Did I imagine it or did players, when they had fallen over, jump up more quickly? I'm not sure. But of one thing I was sure. We won. Two-nil.

As I drove away I thought that my sessions with the players were turning into psychiatric group therapy. I arrived home and stopped the car, Jim ran inside but I sat there thinking. In group therapy the participants talk about each other and criticise each other. And they all talk about the most awful things that occur to them and often wallow in that mire.

But I had forbidden that sort of thing in my group. Quite the opposite. Criticism was not "on". Not of anybody. Including me. I thought: Group Therapy With No Negatives. Then I said something rude to myself. A rough translation would be, "John, get your feet back on the ground. Who do you think you are?"

I stepped out of the car and put both feet on the ground. The ground felt like a good place for them.

Game 35

CONCENTRATION AND THE BACK PASS

We had won three out of the last four games and the players were getting their act together and having a lot of fun. It was beginning to look as though winning was even better than they thought it would be. It was more fun than they had anticipated. A lot more fun than always losing.

An incident occurred a few minutes before half-time. We were defending just a few metres from our own goal. One of our players had the ball. His options were to pass to his team-mate on his right or to his goalie on his left. The opposition were closing in fast, two of them. If our player passed to his team-mate then the problem was that we were still under attack by two of the opposition and possibly more approaching. But that was by far the easiest option. Instead he passed it to our own goalie and in doing so the ball passed within about 30 centimetres of an attacking opposition boot. Everyone watching gasped as our goalie collected the ball safely up in his arms and stood there. The game momentarily stopped and then our goalie gave the ball a big kick right down the side of the field and the crisis was over, the game went on.

Half-time whistle. The score was even at one goal each. They were eating their oranges and had formed a group and looked up as I came over to join them. I said, "Who did that back pass right near their striker?"

In a flash I realised that my voice was stern and forbidding. In a microsecond I could hear myself in times long gone saying, "What a stupid thing to do, it nearly cost us a goal."

A tentative hand went up and a quiet voice said, "Me."

I had their undivided attention. What was I going to say? I said, "*Fantastic*. What concentration!" Wide eyes. I went on, "How incredibly exciting." Big smiles. "And what nerves of steel."

I bit into an orange half and they talked excitedly among themselves about the back pass and the game generally. They went onto the field and in the second half put another goal into the net and won the game two to one.

I ruminated on how I had changed. How could I have been so dumb? In the bad old days I would surely have abused them for taking a risk with that back pass, even if it had worked. My God, if it had failed I would have shouted at them and tried to humiliate the perpetrator of the foul deed. Incredible. Excitement was one of the best parts of the game! How things had changed. Especially me.

Game 36
MAKING A GOAL, SCORING A GOAL

The result of the last game — game 35 — set me thinking. It was, firstly, a game. That meant (to me) that it had to be fun or nobody would play. Well, not quite. Some people play games for reasons other than fun, but the operative word seemed to be "play". Which was different from, say, "work".

That brought me to an interesting conclusion. If I could devise a system that was successful in a play situation, would the same system (or a slightly modified version) work in a "work" situation? I recognised that I was not on the field when the team were winning. I was not making them win, which was what I initially thought would have to be the case. When we were losing, though, it was me that was making them lose. My position, now that they were winning, seemed to be to organise things so that the team could win without fear or anxiety and in an environment where they were motivated to excel themselves.

My tools were words. They certainly were not football skills. Just words. In my search through the city bookshops for the book that would unlock the secrets of the (soccer) universe I bought a book called *Crazy Talk, Stupid Talk* by Neil Postman. I recommend it to anyone who works with words, although soccer coaches might find it boring. The book set me thinking about scoring goals.

Goals are usually scored by the "strikers" who, in the line-up, are the front row. If there are three of them they might wear shirts numbered 9, 10 and 11. If one of them scores a goal he is applauded. I thought that the concept of one player scoring a goal seemed to fly in the face of the whole team concept. Surely the team scores all the goals. The striker might be the last player to touch the ball. But so what?

The previous week I had been prompted to try and analyse goal scoring. Although we had won, we nearly scored an extra goal. One of our strikers, Sean, was lining up to shoot into the left-hand side of the net from about 15 paces out. Coming up fast alongside Sean, five paces or so to his right, was his team-mate striker, Dylan. The goalie was moving over defensively in front of Sean. I thought of calling out, "Pass the ball to Dylan" but I was too far away and also shouting instructions in a moment of intense concentration is a stupid thing to do.

In the "split second that really matters" Sean kicked the ball at the net — straight into the hands of their goalie. Some of our spectators clapped — they were applauding the good run and the near-goal — and the game went on. I thought Dylan had been in a much better position to score than Sean, but Sean must have wanted to score the goal himself. His personal ambitions must have been bigger than his team ambitions. Dylan, on the other hand, had seen Sean going forward. Instead of (as in the old days) standing there to watch Sean, Dylan had run. He had run very fast — he had no ball at his feet to slow him down — and was overtaking Sean at the vital moment.

It was the perfect move, as it threatened the goalie with an attack from two directions. There was another opposition player between our players and the goal but he was not a threat to us scoring. My immediate reaction was that Sean was being selfish. *Wrong*. We won the game anyway, and by this time I had a rule: the only things I said after a game were going to be these: If we won — lavish praise. If we lost — "It's only a game" or something similar. *No criticism after the game*. If something of a critical nature really needed to be said it could wait until training night. By then I would have thought of a way of saying it so that it did not sound like a criticism, or emotional. Emotions were for winning, never for losing.

So at training night after game 35 I talked and practised strategies for scoring goals. I stressed that the full-backs were just as important as the last player to touch the ball when we scored a goal. I said that with a well-planned goal that resulted from several passes, the last player to touch the ball was sometimes the *least* important player. His job was sometimes the easiest.

A couple of the top scorers looked a little piqued. I said, pointing to the top scorers, "They get enough claps from the spectators, so don't feel sorry for them. But I think the *real* hero is the person who *makes* the goal. This is a team game. When we score a goal, very often the player who *makes* the goal is the second last or the third last player to touch the ball. But every player in this team wins when we win. The strikers just get the glamour. Everyone here is on this team, right? And last week this team *won!*" Murmurs of assent.

The best part of all was that when I said things to the group I was not getting that old glazed eyes look. I didn't want to see that look again—so I kept everything as brief as possible. I was constantly on guard against falling in love with the sound of my own voice. I thought about what I was going to say before I said it, and then kept it as short as I could.

Saturday came. Game 36. It worked. Players seemed to be backing each other up more. We won two to nil.

Game 37

More Positive Thinking

A lot has been written about Positive Thinking. It is sometimes called "Dale Carnegie-ism" and this is usually meant in a derogatory way. It often has connotations of sales meetings where the salesmen all get around singing and psyching themselves up into a kind of trance. If that is how you think about it then you should try to resolve the situation. Divide Positive Thinking into two distinct categories: the kind you dislike, and the other kind, which we are talking about here.

Find a new name for the kind of Positive Thinking you dislike. Try "witchdoctor-hype". Of the two kinds there is only a small overlap where similarity occurs. Ignore the overlap. Regard Positive Thinking in a technical sense only. For example: a knife sticking out of someone's back is a dreadful murder weapon. The same knife may be great at chopping up onions for making a delicious meal. The knife itself can be regarded technically and is not involved in either occupation except as a tool. It is just a knife. It doesn't have a mind of its own. It does not know what you call it.

Positive Thinking has an interesting function. First, consider Technical Thinking. Like driving a car. That is, normal driving, from one place to another, competently operating the controls and obeying all the road rules. A technical operation with no emotions, no goodness or badness having any relevance. Then, over the Technical Thinking part in your brain imagine you could put a protective cover of Positive Thinking, which acted like a wall, a cover, a protective device. It would prevent the fog of anything, such as the Fear of Anxiety and Losing, spreading over your brain and distorting the Technical Thinking. The driving analogy is valid.

Car accidents are often caused (half the time, anyway) by a fog overlaying a brain that is trying to drive the car using Technical Thinking. Alcohol of course is the big killer. But a heated argument can cause a driver to go out onto the road in a very angry frame of mind and drive recklessly. And dangerously.

Positive Thinking can act as a protective device. First of all it must have a positive name; like the bad sort of Positive Thinking, the good sort should have a name. You are looking for a name that is going to protect your brain from deadly emotional fogs. The name can be anything but it must be positive to the person using it.

A good positive name is "fun". But the positive word must be right for you. For example, I have seen the word "win"— for some a positive word—cripple a person's performance. So you must choose your own. And if you are coaching a team you must choose a word that suits everybody on the team. The coach talking to the team *creates* the semantic environment for the team and defines the words and their meanings so everyone understands what is meant all the time.

A negative word such as "lose" can overlay the brain with influences just as powerful as a full bottle of Scotch whisky or an uncontrollable tearaway temper. Negative Thinking interferes with the neuromuscular signals from the brain to the muscles. It can literally trip a running player. Positive Thinking does not. Obviously here we are playing with words—the game called semantics. And every game of soccer is played in a semantic environment of its own.

It is quite exciting to conspire with a group and say things like, "Now when Oscar says 'Oscar' he is saying to everyone to leave the ball for him to gather. Maybe get in the way of the opposition but don't try to take the ball itself."

I said, "Go on Oscar, try it out." Oscar had a ball. He bounced it once on the ground in front of him—caught it— held it out and said, "Oscar—my ball. Oscar's ball." Everybody smiled. He hugged the ball. I said, "You win an Oscar for that performance." Loud groans.

One interesting negative name that I have seen written on

the faces of players more times than I would wish is "Here come those big bastards who are going to kick our shins and knock us to the ground". It is often shortened to "Here come those big bastards". This almost always results in a losing game, even if the players who are thinking it are highly skilled and extremely tough. The losing run of play in the game then reinforces the negative thinking which becomes a self-fulfilling prophecy—big bastards always win.

The way to protect the players' brains from external influences is with Positive Thinking. The singing salesmen type of Positive Thinking (witchdoctor-hype) can also work in this way. So don't reject it out of hand all the time. It does sometimes work.

If you don't like singing salesmen, well that's OK. I don't. Some people think they are totally uncivilised. A barbaric kind of war chanting. They are (of course) entitled to that view and to cherish it. The Positive Thinking in this book can be unrelated to war chants except that it sometimes achieves the same results.

There is a body of opinion that holds that a little fear or anxiety at the right time and the right place can produce a little extra in performance. I used to think so. Not any more. At least not for me and certainly not for my team. Game 37 was played in winter sunshine. We won one goal to nil.

Game 38

OVER THE TOPS OF OUR HEADS

Game 38 was an away game. We were defending our goal with slight panic instead of measured calm and in the heat of the moment one of our players, Eric, put his hand out and stopped the ball. Hand ball. Penalty. Against us.

A penalty is a free kick from a spot in front of the goal and usually results in a goal. Briefly a penalty is awarded for foul play *on* an attacking player in front of the goal.

Eric sometimes played goalie and in the heat of the moment forgot that he was an ordinary player and went to grab the ball with his hands. The opposition player placed the ball for the penalty kick and stepped back a long way. Run, bang, up very fast, rising, and away clear over the top of the net and into the trees, no goal. Phew. Half-time whistle.

Eric was distraught. He was saying, "Sorry . . ." even before we settled into our oranges. I said, "Hey, forget it. Happen to anyone. It's just a game. Even if they had scored, can't be helped." I looked around and pointed at all the other players. "Anybody can make a mistake, can't they!" and a couple volunteered, "Sure thing" and similar remarks. I said it with sufficient conviction that would ensure Eric was not criticised by another player. I hoped. Change the subject quickly. "A great game," I said. The score was nil-all.

Eric played on the wing in the second half. I wondered if he would be affected or not. I certainly had not heard any player say anything to him about the penalty kick he gave away. The play was down near the opposition goal and the ball rolled — not very fast — over to Eric. There were about eight players between him and the opposition goal, and their goalie was moving out towards Eric.

And then it happened. Eric took two or three measured steps and kicked the ball with a chipping motion and a beautiful follow-through like a high-kicking gymnast. High. Higher, in a perfect parabola, and as every pair of eyes followed it, down it came, over everybody, just under the cross-bar and into the net! I screamed from the sidelines, *"Fantastic!"*

As the ball went into the net Eric ran three or four quick paces and jumped into the air. Both his arms and legs bent back like a ballet dancer as he whooped for joy. I have the sight permanently in my mind in a kind of "freeze-frame". It is labelled "fun".

The final score—a win—one to nil. I knew that in one player at least I had satisfactorily suppressed the fear and anxiety of making mistakes.

Eric was very slight, a lightweight. A certain candidate for the dreaded "Here Come Those Big Bastards" syndrome. And yet here he was totally free of it and showing superb skill and laughing, within minutes of making a blunder. A blunder that used to be the embarrassing kind. Not any more. We had reduced it to a silly little mistake. The kind anybody might make.

Game 39
WHAT TO DO WHEN THE BALL IS FAR AWAY

The most important thing to do is to keep active. If a player has nothing physical to do then mental activity is essential as a barrier against any kind of thinking that might produce anxiety. The mind should be filled so that there is no room for any unwanted thoughts. One obvious way to do this is tactical thinking.

The champion tennis player, Martina Navratilova, said, "I don't seem to have time to get worried or nervous. The reason is I am so busy thinking about tactics and my play."

If you are trying to *not* think about your opponent you are probably wasting your time, especially if such thoughts have attained a certain level of intensity in your brain. Like that glorious legal phrase sometimes uttered by judges, "I would direct the jury to ignore that (often startling piece of) evidence and pretend they did not hear it." For instance, if you are running onto the field to face a team like Liverpool it would be ridiculous to say to yourself, "I will not give them the rough treatment because they are little sissies."

What happens in such games is that a low level of anticipation and a high level of respect is in most players' minds regarding the opposition. As the game progresses there comes into being a critical level — like a critical weight of uranium in a bomb — when, for instance, the opposition scores the first goal. Boom. The fallout in your own team — adrenalin, fear of failure, aggression, anger with team-mates, and a desperate character — often comes into the play. Your team kicks more wildly, less accurately, overloaded with adrenalin and uptight thoughts.

The cure? The players must fill their minds with tactics

and strategies so that the deleterious thinking about the opponents is kept subcritical by sheer activity of available "brain-space". Make the tactics flexible enough to meet any situation. This means total concentration by the players no matter how the game goes. Protect their thinking with a shell that has a name like: "We are not dealing with life and death, we are involved in a game. We are not jumping out of the trenches and killing the opposition with bayonets. We are playing a game of skill."

These techniques seem to remove the dreaded responsibility fears that interfere with muscle control.

Game 39 was, above everything else, fun. We won five goals to two. Every goal we scored caused our players to leap into the air like dancers.

An ex-rugby-playing father said, "John, these kids aren't playing football. They're more like a mob of poofter ballet dancers." He was smiling while he spoke. His son was an active member of our winning team.

Every goal scored by the opposition caused our players to talk a little to each other about strategy as they ran back to their "kick-off" positions on the field. Not depressed talk about the opposition scoring. Active tactical talk about what to do about it.

At training (on the following week night) we played against another team under the lights. I talked to them about holding their positions when the ball moved to the other end of the field. I said, if the ball is not near you then here is what you must do. Don't just stand around. Look about you and notice where all the other players are, where the open space is; where the goal is. Know where everything is so that if the ball comes your way unexpectedly you will know where you are without having to take your bearings. Signal to each other about your positions. Keep busy.

It was a good week.

Game 40

GALA DAY NUMBER TWO

The end of season game. Gala Day was held on a large field which comprised several soccer fields, and several games were played at once. Knockout contests were held. If a team lost once they were out of the competition. If there were eight teams then the winners would play three games (eight in the first round, four in the second round, two in the final).

With eight of our last nine games won I was feeling pretty confident. I organised my brain as I wandered about the field talking to players and their picnicking families. A team that plays a 40 per cent game loses. Hopefully, I seemed to have a system that lifted their game above the 50 per cent mark and they won. Tops on and gather around for the first game of the Gala Day contest.

Our opposition were short of players. Their coach, a sad-looking woman, I knew. Her husband had deserted her and his soccer team! She had been left with her two children, the mortgage, and inherited a soccer team, and a fairly poor one at that!

I addressed our group. "They are a nothing team, they haven't even got enough players. Are there any volunteers to play on their side and make a game out of it?"

Silence. "Come on—it's just a game, you guys. Won't someone help them out?"

Two hands slowly went up. "Oh, no!" objected some players. The two volunteers were good players, one of them very good. "We can't play without Sean."

I said, "Just for this game. We can't lose. And everybody plays for us in the other games." They were apprehensive.

I said, "They have hardly won a game all season. Go on, give it a go."

"Oh, OK," said the main objectors.

It was a fun match.

Sean's father was cheering Sean instead of either of the two teams. Then he would cheer our team if we were getting a bit slack. He got some funny looks from Sean who was really enjoying himself. Sean scored for the opposition. They would not have done much without him.

We won the match two goals to one and everyone had a good time. We lost the next match which put us out of the contest.

But what a season we had had. As I walked around among the players and their families it was completely the opposite to my memories of my previous Gala Day. Then I had been overcome with feelings of depression and of having let the team down. This time, as I walked about, all I could see were friendly faces. We had had a jolly good season. I handed out the club medal to each player and they looked at them like the Legion of Honour. A happy day.

Game 41

NEW SEASON:
THE BENEVOLENT DICTATOR

Spring had come and gone and now summer was fading. It was time for the ball game. Down to the park and teams were sorted out. A new season. Mostly old faces, some new.

How different it was for me. After two seasons (nearly) starting with heart-in-mouth dread here I was eager to go! I had talked to Harry over the summer and told him how great soccer was. The odd player that I saw seemed keen, too.

A few players had left — and there were a few new ones. Membership would not settle down for a few weeks as players changed teams or perhaps where they lived.

Before the first day I read some of my notes from last season. They made interesting reading. Most of them are here and you have read them already. The one that struck me was about forcing the players to be friendly to each other, even if they were not so disposed naturally. It was a dictatorial thing to do. I had just demanded that everybody be friendly. If they didn't like it — out. Play in another team. No question of fair or unfair. A plain edict.

In one of the books on business management I read that the Hewlett Packard computer company had very little duplication of research because of a high level of trust between the researchers. If one researcher told another about his work he trusted the other not to misuse the information in any way. So nobody went around stealing other people's ideas to claim them for their own. Personal glory was sublimated for cooperation and resulting team glory. The precondition was a high level of trust. It worked; the company is very successful.

I wondered how to get players to trust each other without having to wait years for it to evolve and grow. I decided to try the dictator method, in the same way I had demanded that all the players be friendly. There was no room for discussing about it, I just insisted. Never before had I done anything like it — to lay down the law like that to a group. Thou Shalt Be Friendly. Thou Shalt Trust Thy Neighbour. Well, I had the power of a dictator. While we were winning.

It was a strange world I had talked myself into. The power I had was the same as when I had a team that never won at all, but now I could walk up to a player and say, "You apologise to that guy and tell him you are sorry and that it won't happen again. And now shake hands. And look him in the eyes. And no more of that bullshit. Or go and play in some other team." And it all happened. It worked like magic. When my team lost all the time the player may have walked out on me. I felt like Batman and Robin. A force for good.

There was excitement as we kicked the almost unfamiliar ball around the field. A bit of limbering up. A little sprinting. A little paperwork with names and addresses. We started off with "pig in the middle". A circle of players and one player in the middle trying to get the ball.

Game 41. The players were all early for the first match of the season. Two new players on the team. Two reserves. Nobody absent. I told four they would only be able to play half a match each — change at half-time. I also told them there was nothing personal about it and everybody would have to take turns at half a match when we had too many players. I said it did not mean they were the worst players on the team. They were members of the team but we had to have reserves to accommodate sickness and such.

It was a home game and by half-time we were winning by one goal to nil. I looked at my watch just before half-time and suddenly realised I was getting anxious! I went into an immediate huddle with myself. I stopped calling out to the players and thought about the half-time break. The half-time break came and by then I was calm. And happy. What the hell did it matter if we lost a game of soccer for goodness' sake? I shifted into my psychiatrist mode.

I asked them how the game was going and they gave pretty

happy answers. "Going to score some more goals?" I asked, "or are you going to move back into defence and make do with the one goal and just stop them getting a goal."

A couple of voices said, "Score some more" but without great conviction. Most of all they did not seem anxious at all, so I just kept asking them how they felt about the game and went over a few good moves that they had made. Back onto the field and away they went. They came near to scoring several times but another goal was not forthcoming. But neither did the opposition score. Our goalie had only one or two touches of the ball all the second half. We won the first game of the season one to nil.

"See you all at training, Group," I said as they departed smiling.

Game 42
PSYCHOLOGICAL STRATEGIES

The psychological strategies are a little like a recipe that needs cooking a different way every game. Or perhaps with different ingredients. Both the ingredients and the cooking vary with the wind, the weather, the time of day and the mood of the group. Not to mention the make-up of the opposition team. Which is possibly why some famous coaches are natural winners, they have a natural talent for assessing all the factors of each game.

However the following ingredients are basic.

1. Get the main objective of the game defined and agreed on by every player. The most famous saying (and one that I personally disagree with) is a famous American coach who said that, "Winning isn't everything—it is the *only* thing." I was having maximum success with: "We are here to have fun playing a game. It doesn't matter if we win or lose as much as it matters if we don't have any fun." Pause. "And the best fun is winning!" (Affirmative murmurs from the group.)

2. The coach then must assume responsibility for the results and whether the objective is achieved or not. Fun, as the objective, was my favourite for this particular group, but presumably other objectives will work as long as they are mutually agreed on.

3. Remove all fears and anxieties. One of the main barriers to seeing yourself as a winner is anxiety about the unknown. Have a storehouse of light-hearted non-barrier openings for when you arrive at the game. Some examples: (a) "Is this their (the opposition's) first game of football?" (b) "Do they look a bit miserable?" (c) "Has anyone ever heard of their team?" (A risky one if they happen to be Liverpool!) (d) "Now this

match should be an easy one to win, but that does not mean players are to take it easy. It means we can have fun playing the game."

4. Have no internal competition. Establish a clear difference between internal and external competition. The most startling revelation (to me) was that the fast players in our winning team did not resent the slower players as long as the slow ones were doing their best. (I do not mean quite hopeless players; happily we had none, ours were all normal.) No internal competition means that if you are passing to a fast team-mate you put the ball a fair way in front of him as he runs towards it; passing to a slower player means you allow for the fact without resenting his slowness. In both cases (of course) the ball finds its mark — just where your team-mate wants it.

5. Raise your personal credibility to a very high level. Do this using an applied psychology technique. Say, "You can do it!" then use the high credibility generated to get the player to do the type of play that you want — within (of course) the limits of the player's ability and circumstances. The play could be a particular move like a back pass or a header or a planned move from a free kick (called a "set piece").

6. They do it. (However major or minor.)

7. Use the fact of them doing it to keep your credibility at a very high level. This positive reinforcement of their capabilities is known as "using cybernetics in a win loop".

8. Always tell the truth. Poetic licence (otherwise known as slight exaggeration) is OK especially in a happy environment, but never transparent flattery.

9. Never take the credit for winning, always say (with total truth) that the players won the game. This was brought home to me after we won game 42. One of the players' parents came up to me smiling after the game. He had seen some of the play. He said, "Wow, John, your players have improved out of sight!" They certainly had. I said so at great length. Thank goodness he did not mention my coaching.

10. Don't care too much. That builds apprehension in your own mind, and then it shows. And like a fertile virus it infects

the players. Place a total quarantine against the deadly infections of worry and despair.

11. Address the problem of how to think of yourself (that is, each player thinking of himself) as a winner — especially if you have never won! It *can* be done. Here is how. Never mind history, common sense, reality, or people's opinions. Accept yourself (as a player) as average or normal. That is not so hard to do. Next, accept that no matter how good or bad you are there will always be someone who has a self-esteem rating either lower or higher. If you can think of the opposition as having a lower self-esteem than yourself, then no problem; you don't need to think about them much at all, think about tactics and so on. If the opposition have a higher self-esteem than yourself then you have to "get under their guard". Think of them with their noses in the air and their chests stuck out and don't think of defeating them in a head-on confrontation. Think of outwitting them. Their pride (real or imagined) can make a wonderful environment in which to operate your plans for the game.

Game 42 was the second game of the season. Most of the players had arrived early, which lifted my spirits for the coming season. I talked about the above recipe for winning. Two minutes before kick-off I said, "There is an old Chinese proverb: 'Even the worst of us can serve our fellow man as horrible examples.'" A second or so of doubt as they wondered if I was going to criticise a player.

I pointed, "Well there are some horrible examples out on the field; go and show them how the game of soccer should be played."

We did. We won two to nil.

Game 43

PASS TO A TEAM-MATE
WHO EXPECTS TO WIN

The vital aspect of the game of soccer is the pass of the ball from one player to another. And the ball can be passed quicker than any human can run.

Now, imagine you are passing the ball to a very fast but very selfish player. Imagine he has just told you you are as wet as water. (Say you just did a rather poor kick.) Just pretend that he is the obvious choice of player to pass the ball to. Imagine if you are tempted to kick it ahead of him but maybe almost too far ahead of him. Such are the Forces of Darkness. Imagine the awful possibility that you could find yourself saying to him under your breath, "You're so smart, there, get that . . ." and kicking the ball just out of his reach. Or the possibility of passing the ball to him instead of ahead of him.

Imagine you are receiving the ball. You are running towards the opposition goal and your team-mate is passing the ball to you and you will race ahead with the ball at your feet. The difference between our team now they were winning and the team that lost all the time was about a full second or more in a running attack. Instead of expecting a pass to be made directly towards them, players were now expecting to pick up the ball on the run and well ahead of them. And in a second a player can travel about six metres!

The game was assuming a different character to me. The goals still only took a very short time to "take place". A few seconds in an hour. But it wasn't just a few lucky seconds. The game was the game and the few seconds came at the end of a section of the game. After the goal the game was not so much continued but rather re-started. So each goal was a kind of mini-game and a signal for another game of fun to commence. Looked at this way, each mini-game was of very different length, but had a beginning, a middle and an end and an unambiguous objective—a goal.

A pass to a player who is not going to win is probably or possibly fairly directly towards him. A pass to a player who is going to win is ahead of him. (Unless of course he is standing still!) There is an added technical advantage as well. The nearest opposition player has to do a quick mental triangulation, he has to watch both the player and the ball at the same time but they are quite likely to be in different directions from him. This often gives him a small amount of inertia. A small but very vital amount.

Game 43 was a winner. The score was four to one. There was a great feeling in my soul of an exciting season unfolding. As I drove Jim home I led him in a duet of loud singing. (I feel slightly self-conscious naming the song. It was "We Are the Champions".)

Game 44
THE WALL PASS

I spent the week reading every moment I could. I had several books on the game of soccer (as well as my growing library of applied psychology books) and bought more, reread some. I read with a new enthusiasm. I tried to see just where anything I had learned about popular psychology could mean looking at soccer tactics in a new or interesting way. I was thrilled to find — it could!

I discovered that Hungary beat England six to three at Wembley in 1953. Many people became convinced that the Hungarians had developed some sort of telepathy. What they had really developed was a new way of playing the game. Basically it involved patterns of play — predetermined — and teams within a team. And starting with the basic move consisting of two players and the wall pass.

The wall pass has a beautiful simplicity about it. It seems to have been developed in the 1930s and quickly adopted by all the European countries. The wall pass is played like this: player A passes to player B who acts like a wall, and he bounces the ball directly back to A again. But with a vital ingredient added. After A has kicked the ball he moves. In other words B kicks the ball to where A will be . . . the pattern is thus a triangle. A kicks the ball to B who is stationary. (Not that he needs to be.) As soon as A has kicked he runs. If A is already running then his best move is to change direction after he has kicked the ball. B watches first the ball and second A. He does a one-touch kick (like a wall) of the ball so the ball goes to a point on the field, it arrives at the point at the exact moment A arrives at the same point.

Why is the wall pass so successful? Everybody (nearly) is watching the ball. They take their eyes off A and follow the ball on its way to B. Not only players, but most spectators do the same thing. As A scoops up the ball he has a good turn of speed already going for him (and he has the ball in his possession), but he has nobody immediately chasing him. The opposition players are mostly overloaded with momentum from lurching first this way and that — towards B and then away from him. A well-worked wall pass is lovely to watch. It is the three-card trick, the pea and the thimble. Now you see it and now you don't. We are all taught to watch the ball. Follow the ball with your eyes. Never take your eyes off the ball. Players, spectators, the referee.

I tried to teach the group the wall pass. I failed. I tried some more, but all the other players standing around knew what was going to happen and there was no surprise at all! I became frustrated. Eventually I got them playing "pig in the middle" but with an important difference. I organised the play with only three players trying to keep the ball away from one player, and I marked out an area with markers, a circle or a square. Then they often had to pass the ball back from whence it had come. They had no option but to practise the wall pass! It started to work.

Psychologically the effect on the team was incredible, but totally unexpected. They failed to master the wall pass very well, but every once in a while (in the now usual night-time friendly game with another training team) our players passed the ball back to its source with a single kick. Sometimes the original player had moved. There was advantage, although not as much as there should have been, in the play when they did it. The real advantage was that their morale just soared into the sky.

In game 44 it worked like a conspiracy of fun and games. We won three to one.

As we were gathering our things together after the game, our spirits very high, Harry Radds came over. His team was to play on the same field after us and he had been watching us win. He said, "Gee you've got some good players on your team." I had heard the exact phrase before. I gave the same response as always. I said, "Have we ever!"

Game 45

THE SEMANTIC ENVIRONMENT

The pre-game talks were turning into group therapy sessions without the criticism of psychiatric groups. I read several psychology books during the week. The effect on me was as much or more than the effect on our team's play. I understood that I was in a particular semantic environment — a world of words. Every little piece of communication could have a function and the surest way to waste time was to give a boring lecture. So I endeavoured to get to the point with a minimum of fuss. Some examples:

1. You are playing in that direction (pointing) and the wind is behind you. So the higher you kick the ball the further it will be carried by the wind. Allow for the wind for every kick except perhaps short kicks along the ground. For a big kick that you want to go far, think about getting underneath the ball with your boot.

2. Now the wind is against you. Two things. Firstly, don't kick the ball high, keep it low to the ground. Secondly, dribbling. When you are dribbling with the ball you have the advantage of the ball sticking close to your feet. It means you can run faster with less danger of tapping the ball away from you.

3. There is no wind and the sun is behind you for this half. You will have a much better view of the ball than the opposition. They will be dazzled if you kick the ball high. Lots of nice lobs, please. And for the second half — playing into the sun — keep the ball low.

In short, it is possible to look at anything, yes anything, in a positive way. Sun, wind, anything.

How about being a player short? Yes! Eyes very wide.

If we are a player short, that is we only have ten players instead of 11, the opposition can become over-confident. They are sure to see you are a player short, so why not tell them yourselves? Instead of the natural tendency to keep it a secret, boast about it! And when they are over-confident they are vulnerable. And when our players become aware of these factors they can become winners. Think of it like this — 10 per cent of our team missing is of no consequence when you think we are 10 per cent better than the opposition to start with. And when the opposition players are getting in each other's way, we will be more spread out! There is no limit to thinking about every aspect of the game in a positive way.

For a positive thought to work well, often it is best considered in isolation. Do not consider it in an academic or balanced or fair way at all. Emotions and not logic are involved. I divided my planning into two kinds, emotional and tactical.

For tactical planning all the facts need to be considered. The plan needs to be worked out with all possible contingencies. For emotional planning only the positive aspects should be considered. And they should present a pleasant and interesting way of channelling the players' concentration on the game.

I started the pre-game talk with tactical planning, and at half-time got into the emotional (psychological) kind. I spent three or four minutes only on each kind. At half-time the score was one goal each. It was a great game, no dirty play, all good clean fun. But the opposition was a good team. Maybe as good as ours. By the final whistle the score was unchanged. A draw. Never mind. Nobody seemed depressed about it.

HOW I COACHED MY TEAM TO VICTORY

Game 46
THE TV GAME ANALOGY

I was walking through the city and passed a TV game arcade. Row after row of people pressing buttons and manipulating joysticks with their eyes concentrating on the TV screen in front of them. I thought I had better have a new look at the games in the light of my newly acquired knowledge. The scores were big numbers. Obviously the makers figured that the players did not want to win a point or two. They wanted to win hundreds, thousands and even tens of thousands. With some of the games the smallest score was a thousand.

I can't do anything about that regarding soccer. The score rate inhibits my group from scoring 10,000 goals in the one game. And then I noticed the link to my soccer thinking. All the games had an "enemy". Whether the enemy was space ships or martians or a dragon, there had to be an enemy to get past or destroy (with a laser) to win the points. Well, there wouldn't be much fun in playing a game of soccer without an opposition team. Maybe some fun, but not a lot.

That was it! That was how to think of the opposition teams! Just as obstacles on an obstacle course. I felt enlightened. Soccer was not a flat race like athletics or a horse race. It was an obstacle race. Or a TV game. And you didn't win a TV game by being hard or aggressive or violent. You won by being clever. You watched how the machine reacted and you behaved accordingly. You did not play by formula or a fixed game plan. Your strategy had to flow with the tide, bend with the wind without breaking. It had to suit the nature of the obstacles and get around them. The best you could plan was in the nature of mini-plans, mini-strategies for small sequences in the play, and then change the plan depending on how the opposition was behaving. That was the clue. I was thrilled by the discovery. The oppposition was not something to beat or get beaten by, but obstacles to get around.

Game 46. I said, "Can everybody play TV games?" You can guess the rest. I told them my theory, how there just wouldn't be a game at all if there were no opponents. I told them that the opposition players were the obstacles in an obstacle race. I told them that we did not win because we were bigger. (They shook their heads, muttering, "Not bigger.") Or faster. A smart-mouthed player said, "Slower?" and I raised my arm in mock threat to pound his head. Or angrier. No communications gap. Every player listening. I pointed to my skull with my forefinger. Several players did the same. "We use our brains," I said. Smiling faces and muttered voices, "Brains."

We talked some strategies, I changed some players' positions and they ran onto the field. Did we win? We did indeed.

If it had been a TV game the score would have been a million. It was soccer. We won five to one. I patted them on their backs as they came off, and all I could say, over and over, was, "Fantastic, fantastic."

Game 47
No Internal Competition

With so many wins to our name I began to take more and more notes on what was happening and also I thought I should check out what the other coaches were saying to their teams. Mainly, I wondered, were the successful coaches saying the same things I was? I figured that it may not be easy to find out, because if they were anything like me they talked to their teams in total privacy. They certainly would not want anyone listening in to what they said. I certainly didn't.

Wrong. Not only did they conduct their talks in almost public situations, a thing that I absolutely never did — but sometimes humiliated players in front of other players — and they seemed to do it often. I was amazed. Especially as one of the coaches who shouted a lot had a very successful team.

I puzzled over this for many nights. I looked it up in books. I tried to work out how the players could give of their best after being vilified in front of the rest of the team. Well, I guess there are a thousand ways to skin a cat.

I didn't really pick up the style of this particularly successful coach at first. His name was Charlie. I wandered about the field on training nights observing as much as I could. When we were having a friendly game with another local team at night and I was not the referee, I sometimes asked a question of a more experienced coach. I spoke to Charlie. I told him my team was doing very well, I actually said we were winning most of our matches, but told him he seemed to know a lot more about the game than I did.

Here is how he worked. Every player in his team was in stiff competition with every other player in the team. In the same team! Any player who did not try hard enough was simply left out of the match at the weekend. Any player who did not try hard enough at training had to run around the field. He actually said to his team, "Well, if training goes well for the first hour and a half then we will have a game for the last half hour." He meant that the game would be a reward.

He told me, "That makes them concentrate, if they train well then after one and a half hours they are just busting for a game. It makes them keen."

One of the training sequences he did was around the goal. He would line up his defenders and the goalie and then he would line up the attackers to try and score a goal. In other words team-mates would be tackling their own team-mates for the ball. And with the coach shouting loudly at them the whole time. It was quite a fearsome sight. But they won most of their matches! Everything seemed to be almost the opposite to what I had found. I had "discovered" that internal competition was a poison to the team spirit, and yet here was a team winning and winning well with the maximum of internal competition. Why?

I don't know. I will not pretend. I never found out and so I do not know still. Perhaps there are really a thousand ways of playing the game . . . But in game 47 our way worked for us again. A one to nil win.

Game 48

NATIONAL TEAMS AND CLUB TEAMS

Game 48 was a draw at one goal each. It was a good game, played against a team similar to our own and played with a good spirit. Both sides enjoyed it and nobody seemed depressed that we had not won. I thought about going over the game and finding out why we had not won. Then I thought, how silly. It had been a good game. You can't win 'em all, John. Fair go. Think about next week. They enjoyed it, didn't they?

Earlier that week, I had watched a national game on TV: England against Scotland. The best players from each country. The best team in each country? Maybe, maybe not. I think not. National teams are usually selected by a selection committee composed of ex-players who choose the best players in the land. And they choose well. But the national teams only play together once in a while. A club team plays together once or twice every week and has training together as well. So a top club team is made up of people who know each other's game like they know their own. They anticipate each other's moves. Sometimes their movements would indicate that they had ESP, or some secret thought transference system.

National teams on the other hand are a collection of star players. Competition between players — the deadly dreaded internal competition — creeps into national teams. If you study a game between countries where the teams are made up of players from many different clubs you will notice that fine edge is missing. More misunderstandings. The pass that is too far ahead or not far enough. In a championship club you will notice what could be called "trust". And players that trust each other are beautiful to watch.

The countries that win World Cups and such are often

composed of small teams within teams. In other words, several of the stars are from the same club team and are used to playing with each other. I knew I did not have a team composed of stars. I had the other kind. The kind that like playing together, that feel they belong. The folklore is that a champion team will usually beat a team of champions.

Game 49

TEASING THE OPPOSITION

Game 49 was a game on our home ground. We were not going well and as half-time drew near I realised I was getting nervous. We had scored but we were losing one to two and the opposition were having most of the "run of play". We looked lethargic. We looked as though we didn't care too much for the game.

I knew better. I knew that the lethargic look often was a disguise for the dreaded losing anxiety syndrome. The depression of losing—even though we were only one goal behind—was slowing the players. Our passes were going straight at our players, instead of ahead of them. I recognised the symptoms. The disease—the losing disease. The cure? Well, I had studied it for long hours over many months. The time had come to see if it will work or not.

The half-time whistle blew. John. Hold your breath. Here we go. "Attention, everybody." There was quiet as they stood around eating their oranges.

"Now, look. We are one goal behind. Do you know what most people think when you are one goal down? They say try harder, run faster, kick harder and so on." I paused. "Bullshit."

I had their attention. Complete silence. Was I going to tell them how to win when you are losing? I held the silence for as long as I could. "Here is how to win."

Another pause, but a short one. "You have to tease them."

No glazing of the eyes. A couple smiled slightly. They liked it. And that meant that it could work. They were all listening with full concentration—a vital prerequisite, not only for listening but also for winning this game.

"Now," and I took three players and positioned them in

a triangle. "This is what you must do. I have the ball, Freddy and Charles are on my team and Bennie is the opposition." I paused while that was absorbed.

"Now my safest pass of course is to Freddy." They all nodded assent.

"Now, if I can pass it to Charles, just out of reach of Bennie, then I am teasing Bennie, aren't I?" I was looking at one or two definite smiles. "Especially if Bennie can *see* I am not making the safe pass to Freddy. Does everybody understand that? Teasing requires massive concentration, and you guys are good at it. If you tease them properly, they are easier to dodge around."

I did a theatrical dodging jump. "If you have the ball and one of their players is coming at you he will be coming fast. Don't panic and get rid of the ball hastily. That's what they will be expecting. No, tease them. Concentrate. Keep your options open until the last split second. Smile. Yes, smile! And smile so everyone can see you. The angrier they get, the faster they run, the more they keep going in a straight line.

"Where you can, pass the ball just out of their reach. And of course the greatest tease of all is if you can lob the ball just over their heads. Pass higher than they could jump to 'head' the ball but not too high. Perhaps so that they could reach up and touch it! But of course that would be 'hand ball' and a free kick to us. They are expecting you to be timid, playing safe, depressed. Being teased is the last thing they are expecting. It will drive them mad."

Eyes lit up. Excitement showed in their faces. They looked at each other and they were smiling. They had a game plan for when they were losing. None of the old nonsense about try harder, run faster, kick further, aggression, attack. None of that at all. "Leave all that aggression to the other team." They had a real plan to work to. And most important of all — they liked it. Several of them were smiling a lot. Some fun was coming their way.

The other team was already moving onto the field, looking full of confidence. They had a winning look. A last word from me (vulgarity, unfortunately, sometimes has a place in the world of words): "Tease the shit out of 'em."

They ran onto the field and took up their positions for the second half. Did it work? It was like a minor miracle. I could hardly believe it. It was the greatest thrill I have ever had coaching. It was more spectacular than our first win.

Our concentration was at absolute peak. Theirs and mine. The opposition would charge at our player who had the ball. Our player would wait until that last moment and make not a desperate kick of blind panic, but a confident, well-controlled pass just out of reach of the opposition. The effect was quite incredible. I shouted with joy. Of course I did not mention the word "tease" when I shouted. That was to be our secret. Well, we did not put 20 goals in that second half. We put two into the net, the opposition put in none and we won the game. A great game.

The effect of our teasing play on the opposition was that it rattled them but not as much as I had anticipated, I suppose. But the effect on our own players was an increase in control over their play. They smiled at each other a lot. We won the game three to two.

The important thing was not that we had won. It was that we had come from behind and won. From being a goal down to winning by one goal. Not particularly incredible as far as the score goes. Winning a game three to two is not front page news. But to me it was. It was the real jump for joy news that applied psychology could work as it was meant to, that is, when you are down. And it was not me tricking the players, not at all; they thought it was a great idea to play it near the opposition, but just out of their reach instead of playing it safe. It was not something underhand or nasty. There was no "aggro". It was a way of blocking the old dreaded depressions with a method that channels the brain into a concentrating mode.

And it worked, it worked. I hugged the players as they came off, or shook their hands. They may have forgotten the plan. They were thinking, perhaps, that they had played a great game, had had a lot of fun playing with their friends, had won the game, and maybe about what was for lunch. I was thinking, also with a lot of joy, that life was not all up and down, black and white. That when you are down there are a thousand ways of getting back up besides the traditional "try harder". And the 49th game plan, oh bliss, oh joy, had been one of them.

Later that week I was watching English soccer on television. Liverpool were losing at half-time. My eyes were concentrating on the screen. They did exactly as my team had done. They did not become more aggressive, kick harder, play more desperately. Not at all. They played as though they were ten goals ahead and playing against the Little Old Ladies Team and were giving a demonstration on how to play the game. They became tricky. They waited until the last split second before passing the ball and instead of playing "safe" they were playing "risky". And they were using the risk factor to put a very fine edge onto their concentration.

Did it work? Yes. They came from behind and won the game. Can I compare a kids' team with the mighty Liverpool? I think so. We had been losing and not dwelling on the fact of it. And we had found a way to overtake the leader in the race and win from behind.

Game 50
THE TWO-SECOND PLAN

I gathered the group around. We were all a bit early for the game and there was plenty of time for a quiet talk.

"Plan what you are going to do for the next two seconds. Then keep updating your plan all the time. The only time your plan will not need updating is if you are not moving and nobody around you is moving. That doesn't happen a lot. Plan what to do if you suddenly get the ball. In a team game most of you, for a lot of the time, do not have the ball. What to do? Just stand around and watch? Never. That is what individuals would do. But a team member can do much more. He can plan and he can look at the positions of his team and the opposition team. The main point is that if your two-second plan does not eventuate then there is nothing lost.

"There is an analogy in 'calling for the ball'. If you call for the ball and the player with the ball does not pass it to you — don't ever think you have wasted your breath calling! If you call convincingly the opposition may think you are going to receive a pass and one or two of their players may move towards you. If that happens — presto — you have thinned out their ranks from where the ball *is* going. You are *all* on this team!

"It is the same with your plan. You may be a fullback, your plan may be to pass the ball out to the wing, nothing happens for a long time, then in a split second the ball is at your feet and you kick it out to the wing without having to stop — you checked out where your winger was a second before you got the ball — and the split second you save saves the goal. The vital ingredient for the two-second plan is to know where every player — both teams — is all the time; particularly the players you can reach with one kick. The time your plan saves can win a game."

I became confidential and lowered my voice. "That is what many teams don't realise. A goal can be scored in a couple of seconds, and a goal can win a game. So you have to know *when* to concentrate. Nobody can concentrate all the time. If the ball is far away from you, save your energy. But your mind doesn't use up energy. Use it to plan all the time. And then, when the moment comes — *go*. If there are three strikers across the field and one of you gets the ball — *all three go!*"

The opposition were moving onto the field. "Here we go. Have fun!" They did. Lots. We won three nil.

HOW I COACHED MY TEAM TO VICTORY

Game 51

THE GLEN HODDLE PLAN

Glen Hoddle can kick the ball a long way and he can kick it very accurately. The Glen Hoddle Plan is based on that and it has won many games for the London team of Tottenham Hotspurs.

A typical plan is to have the Spurs' strikers well onside of the opposition defenders, often spread out in a line across the field. The strikers watch Hoddle. When they see the ball head towards him they get ready. Almost without looking, Hoddle can place the ball in between two of the defenders, and the Spurs' strikers already are running flat out towards the goal, and amazingly one of them collects the ball as he runs.

That plan seems to work once or twice in a game. The time taken? A few precious seconds. Hoddle does not run after the ball a lot. He tries to move into space where there are no players and then waits for his team-mates to pass the ball to him. Then he "earns his wages" with one beautifully accurate kick.

We tried the Glen Hoddle Plan about four times and for three of them our strikers ran offside and the game came to a halt. We placed our biggest kicker in midfield and the strikers were to watch him in anticipation. The fourth time it *nearly* worked. But we had a lot of fun trying to make it work. It seemed to require that the strikers were confident enough to start running even before there was anything to run for.

This was something they had never done in the bad old days. Then they had started their runs much too late—because they "knew" that nobody could "kick that far or that accurately". Having the confidence to start running as the ball was kicked was great.

Even though the plan did not work the spirit of the thing did. We won three to two.

Game 52

CLOUGH, PAISLEY, TOSHACK ET AL.

Famous coaches. Names with a ring of magic to them. Mostly ex-players. All with very sound psychology. Mostly men who play their cards close to their chests. Except perhaps Clough. He never seems to mind telling all. Or what he says is all.

What he says sounds a lot like commonsense. Like, "Nobody can run as fast as a kicked ball." This seems to have been discovered by the Scots about a century ago, and it changed the game fundamentally. It meant that if a player kicked the ball to another player who was unmarked, the receiver had all the time in the world to kick the ball where he wanted to. To paraphrase Brian Clough, "It is not tricks that are used so much as concentrating on the basics, the fundamentals, and doing them exceptionally well."

When I related all this to the group it generated a couple of thoughtful looks. I almost thought I heard, "Hey, yeah!" from a couple of souls. "But not if you muck around wasting time. If you get rid of the ball with a good kick then you know nobody can outpace it."

Did I get through to the group? Perhaps. We won anyway. One nil in a great match.

Game 53

TRUTH IN APPLIED PSYCHOLOGY

Applied psychology suffers from a bad press. One common opinion is that it is trickery and if you detect it being used your defence mechanisms should be quickly put in place. To use it in "real life" it must operate on a base of truth to have credibility. One false note can produce a discord that will negate all worthwhile material.

Game 53 was a loss — the second game we hadn't won that season. (The other was a draw.) We lost two to one. Not too bad by ordinary standards, but our standards were no longer ordinary.

Maybe I shouted too many instructions from the sidelines, maybe I said the wrong thing. We were playing against a crash-hot team and that was probably the real reason we lost. They were highly skilled at every aspect of the game. No doubt they trained twice a week for two or three hours each time and so on and so forth . . . I told myself.

The final whistle had hardly stopped blowing and I could hear Oscar shouting to some of our players, "It's only a game you guys." I almost cried with joy. I could not have put it better myself. He had spoken up because he had heard players complaining about losing. He had heard one player — I don't know which one — making excuses and stating various reasons why we had not won. From my point of view it was great that they were working out for themselves that it was only a game.

We played well against a great team in top form. We nearly won. We had the ball about half the time and it was a very close match. The only thing that I might have done wrong was to shout out too much from the sidelines. And if my shouting betrayed any nervousness then it probably could be detected listening to me. So I resolved to go over what I shouted out and what I should not shout out. Back to the books.

Game 54

THE OPPOSITION IS ARGUING

The game was going well. We were two goals to the opposition's one and our group looked good. Half-time was drawing near. A couple of the opposition players were playing a bit rough. They had become more aggressive as we had gone ahead, and they were looking to kick a few shins. Ours.

I thought about how I would try to tell the guys to keep their cool, not to get hassled by the opposition's aggression. I was thinking about how to put it when I noticed one of the opposition do a bad pass to his team-mate. We got the ball and raced down the field with it. The opposition player who did not receive the ball started to abuse his team-mate.

I immediately thought to tell my guys, "Don't argue among yourselves. The opposition is arguing, and losing." I didn't. I had learned that my immediate instincts were often counterproductive. I thought about what I would say. I lifted my thinking into the Clever Mode. I had a few minutes before the half-time whistle and I thought about what would be the appropriate applied psychology way to say it.

Half-time. Oranges, everybody happy. We were winning two to one. No problems. I didn't say, "Listen everybody . . ." I kept quiet. The one thing I did not want to see was the old glazed bored look of people being lectured. I waited for a little lull in the conversation and then I spoke to a couple of the players, but so that most of them could hear me. Not an announcement, but a bit of "corncob" type wisdom. Sotto voce. I said, "Do you want to know when you have the game well in hand? When you have really got it made?"

Nobody asked but about half the team were listening by then. I said, "When the opposition players are arguing among themselves, that's when." I could have hugged myself. As I spoke I knew I had got it right. If I had said, "Now don't argue . . ." I would have been heading back to the old lecture routine. By restructuring the thing I had put them on top of the problem without waving my fingers.

They immediately started talking about it. "Yeah, I saw one of them kick another one."

"Kick one of us?" I said.

"No—kick his own team-mate!" Another guy said, "Yeah, and one swore at me. Called me a stupid bastard." I did not interrupt the conversation.

It went well. The team was welding itself together without any help from me. "Are they angry?" I said. "Are they ever!" came from our very smallest, lightest player. I was thrilled; he had not the slighest apprehension about any Big Angry Bastards coming at him. He knew he belonged to a team where anger was not allowed. He smiled.

I said, "Let's go" for the second half and they went onto the field.

The final result? We won four to one. I resolved to read more and more. The more I read, the more respect I had for applied psychology and the less I thought of it as trickery. The unusual approach seemed to be so much more powerful than the direct "do this, do that, don't do the other" approach.

Game 55

TRACE ELEMENTS CAN BE POISONOUS ALONE

I wish I could forget game 55. I was slack. Maybe we would have won if I had been on the ball, maybe not. We were up against a very good team.

I arrived at the game feeling "out of it". No preparation. I gathered the group together and told them, "This lot are nothing to worry about. They couldn't win if half of us stayed at home." (Happy laughs from the group.) I said little else. (I didn't feel like talking. Who cared about soccer anyhow.)

Oh, my God how I lied. They were like Manchester United First Division. And it was obvious from the first minute of play. My credibility took a nosedive after another couple of minutes when the ball whistled past our goalie. I won't go over the game. It was very painful. We lost four to nil. We nearly lost about ten to nil. Our players got their act together and battled defensively extremely well, eventually. No thanks to me. I had committed the cardinal sin; I had spouted a bit of "formula" because I was feeling slack and on its own it had been pure poison.

In retrospect? Well, had I known the opposition were a top team I would not have told the group. Never. Anxiety was still the real enemy, not the top team. No, I would have discussed tactics, pure and simple. Who can tell if we would have won or not? Possibly everybody knew that the opposition were a top team except me! All I know is that terrible look on their faces when the opposition scored the first goal. I wished the ground could have swallowed me up. I felt I had betrayed them. I seriously wondered if they would believe me ever again. I said very little at half-time, less after the game. I hoped they would be able to forget it all in one short week.

Game 56

PRAISE AND CRITICISM

Training night and the slaughter of last weekend was still fresh in our minds. "Weren't our full-backs tremendous?"

The group concurred. I mentioned that far from being a bad team, the team we had played last week must be about the best we had played against. More affirmative noises. We went into some training routines. After about an hour of training I knew I had been forgiven.

"I think we would have lost about ten to nil but for our full-backs. They kept their cool. They didn't panic. They just kept sending that ball back from our goal. Oscar took some back passes brilliantly. And if you are under attack and you can keep your cool enough to do good back passes then that is how to play the game. They were a crack team. And I didn't know it. I guess I mixed them up with another team."

"Some mix-up," from within the group. A little wry laughter but the mood seemed good.

"Well," I said, "could we beat them if we played them again?"

"I doubt it," from someone, but they were listening to what I might say.

I went on, "I reckon we might if we used the Glen Hoddle Plan and kept the back line with more players. All the backs in a straight line, all ready to come away from our goal and trap their strikers into playing offside. Let's plan that . . ." and away we went placing players in a good defensive way — one goalie, four in the back line, four in midfield, and only two strikers. We were planning. The main value was not so much in the planning but rather in the fact that we were planning.

It worked. Came the weekend and we won. We started off in the defensive plan but the opposition were a rather weak team and our wingers kept moving forward — in fact everybody kept moving forward. The score line — a three to one victory for us.

Game 57

GOOD LUCK GOALS

Game 57 was played in a light drizzle. The rain made the ground soft and in the pre-game talk I pointed out that no one need feel apprehension about falling over in the wet because the ground was nice and soft. I pointed to some wet patches and suggested to the team that they check out how much more difficult it would be to bounce the ball there. We kicked the ball over the ground to see how much the wet slowed it down. We talked about how much harder it was to kick the ball and about kicking it up in the air around the goal mouth where the ground was muddy.

Onto the field. At half-time the score was one goal each and we were enjoying ourselves. Oranges eaten, not much talk, and back on for the second half.

We had the ball down in the opponent's half and we were looking good. One of our strikers was about 30 metres out and kicked it hard. Four of their defenders were in the way. Two of them touched the ball as it went past. It went in a zig-zag route and hit the side post of the net and went into the goal. Hooray. Our players jumped about for joy. Then a parent — one of our own — shouted out, "That was a lucky goal!" and some of our players turned to look at him as they moved back to the other end for the next kick-off.

I thought, "Luck?" What did luck have to do with it? I was horrified and by the look of them some of our players did not know what to think. Quickly I shouted out loudly, "That's how to play the game you guys." I could see they heard me. "You guys are giving them a lesson on how to play soccer." They heard me. I saw some smiles. The system was working. The parent kept quiet.

Sure, the ball might have been deflected into the goal. But who the hell got the ball up the right end anyway! I had seen some of our players stop congratulating each other when they heard that it was a lucky goal. I had only had a second to realise what the father was doing. It was the perfect example to me of "live" reactive coaching. It was not something that could be anticipated or practised so much as prepared for in a general way. I think I did the right thing in calling out immediately. We put one more ball in the net and won three goals to one.

Lucky goal? Some people are never satisfied. Anything nice happens and they want to compensate for it. They want to balance the situation. I have said to a father, "Your kid played well today," and he has replied, "Yes, but he made some terrible mistakes as well don't forget." Why do some people have to say such compensatory things? I'm not sure. I call the type of person a Compensator. If they won the lottery they would say, "Yes, but $100,000 won't buy what it used to . . ." or "Yes, but I'll have to pay tax on the income . . ." In fact they have to even up whatever is good or great with something bad.

None of that for coaching. And none of it for winning games of soccer either. A goal is a goal. Some have a bit of luck I suppose but so what? That kind of luck seems to spread itself evenly between both sides. (Heaven help the Australian Rules football player waiting for the elongated ball to bounce every which way!)

I had altered my thinking to accept Positive Thinking being free of all that compensation, that evening up, that Yin and Yang, Good and Evil. I thought about the positive things only, and the negative things could wither on the vine, unthought, unwanted, unloved . . .

When the final whistle blew I ran onto the field right in front of the "lucky goal" wet blanket compensating father and shook players' hands and patted backs. Luck? We made our own luck.

Game 58

TRAINING SEQUENCES

Training sequences that did not involve team members tackling each other were the order of the day (actually night). Even though they were breaking records they all concentrated on improving skills such as hitting a target with a well-aimed kick. A favourite was throwing the ball, sometimes along the ground, sometimes bouncing high, within kicking distance of the goal and, at training, players other than Oscar had a turn at being goalie. Another was kicking delicate shots to land in a marked-out square on the first bounce. This was done in two ways. I would throw the ball and the players would kick it to hit the target with the one kick. Then they did the same thing with more time to aim — they could stop the ball and kick with a two-touch movement instead of one-touch.

The most noticeable thing was that although they were winning most of the time they did not think to train less or learn less. Which was very gratifying. It meant that the psychology had a legitimacy, it was based on good play, not just some trick. They were enjoying the training almost as much as the weekend games — and of course they were learning at the same time.

Game 58 we won easily. The score was only three to one but they played with real concentration, and when the goal was scored against them (making it one-all) they did not become the slightest bit bothered.

A player asked me after the game, "How many games to the end of the season, John?"

I said, "Only a couple more. Then you can play cricket for the summer."

Game 59
THE SYSTEM

Does it work? Yes. How?

Like this. An average game is 90 minutes. An average number of goals might be four or six. For 90 per cent of the game the play goes on with no scores made. Sometimes with our team dominating, sometimes not.

Both teams want to win. A team that loses a lot may be holding out for say 45 per cent of the time. For 45 per cent of the time the winning team also play well. For 10 per cent of the time the winning team "get their act together" and put the ball in the net. In other words the final score, say two to nil, polarises the real situation. For much of the game the play may have been more or less even. A truly "one-sided" game (with one team absolutely hopeless) tends to produce scores of something like ten to nil! We had played games like that, but not many. Usually we won or lost three or four goals to one or two.

The System seems to raise the level of play of a team by about 10 to 20 per cent. It does this in two major ways.

1. It increases the teamwork and cooperation of the players which results in a level of play greater than the sum of the individuals. Some people say that this is the true meaning of teamwork. Freedom from fear for the individuals within the team. That is, freedom from the fear of the external forces concentrating on the individual. Specifically, a feeling of "belonging".

2. It raises the level of concentration of individual players.

Combine these factors with appropriate training, tactics and strategies and an ordinary group of players can lift their game above the mediocre and — in the case of my team — to championship level.

Game 59 was really embarrassing. We won it 11 goals to nil. Our opponents were hopeless. I heard later that they had not won a single game all season. I felt sorry for them. My son Jim drew a picture of the game the next day, with the scoreline prominent.

Game 60

GALA DAY NUMBER THREE

The euphoria at the end of the season was not "we have crushed the losers". We were not ecstatic at winning a bloody war. We were from a different semantic environment altogether. I think we all felt the same, the players and myself. We shared a feeling of elation, and a marvellous control over part of our lives; we had shared in something and we had belonged to something, a team. Nothing like a war at all, not life or death. After all, it's only a game.

Gala Day and the fields covered with families and players with lunch and socialising between players and parents. There were lotteries and raffles to raise money for the club, prizes to hand out to teams that had won various competitions and a "knockout" competition for our group. Knockout means lose one game and you are out. That meant a team had to win three games in a row to win the competition. The games were shortened a bit so as not to exhaust the players. Up to eight teams played in the first round, the four winners played the second round, leaving the two finalists in the last round.

We won the first game, two goals to nil, and the second, one to nil. But the grand final was a draw at one to one.

What to do. The officials conferred. Play extra time? No. Both teams were very tired. A penalty play-off. The first team to be two goals ahead of the other would be the winner, penalties to be kicked by all players (not the best kicker in the team) and kicked by each team alternately.

I gathered our group together. Our regular goalie, Oscar, was looking good. And we were allowed to keep the one goalie for all the penalty kicks against us. "OK everyone. Keep cool. Don't worry. Just *concentrate*."

I looked across at the other finalists. Their coach looked worried. I thought, great. (I felt a bit mean, I suppose I hoped he was making his team anxious, just as I used to do many games ago . . .) My last words to my team were, "It's only a game, you guys." Their expressions said, "No it ain't," and they looked positively hyped up, raring to go, go, go. After about six kicks we were ahead two goals and won the knockout competition.

What a day. A European mother of one of our players came up to me. She said, "John you were very lucky to win. You seem much too casual to me. You almost looked as though you didn't care whether they won or lost." I smiled but did not answer.

Our team name was called over the loudspeaker to come to the podium to collect our winners' medals. "There," she went on, "that's what it's all about — *winning*! That's why they play the game! And you look as though you don't even care."

It flashed through my mind to try to explain but I immediately abandoned the idea. I said, "Hannah, I promise you that next year I will try harder."

"Good," she said, as I smiled and made my way to the podium with the players.

What a season. We had lost two, drawn two, and won every other game that we played.

There were a lot of faces smiling at me that afternoon. We'd had a lot of fun playing the ball game. Now for a break for the summer. I thought, a team is a season kind of thing. It is born, it lives, and then the season ends. Maybe that life cycle is part of the magic.

BOOK III
THE TEAM SYSTEM

THE TEAM SYSTEM

The aim of the Team System is to provide a mental environment for the team in which to play the game. The environment must exclude fear and anxiety. It must include cooperation, trust, friendliness, good feelings and the conditions that allow players to concentrate on the play.

The following aspects are listed in alphabetical order rather than order of importance — which varies from team to team.

Action and Reaction: action wins a game, reaction is the defensive play when trying to stop the other team winning. If your players are waiting and then reacting while defending your goal then they are playing in a conservative way. But if they are reacting while they are trying to attack, then they are probably in a losing frame of mind.

For my first 30 games my teams were reacting, and losing. They were concentrating on trying to match their play to the play of the opposition and then in theory beat the opposition at their (the opposition's) own game. This turned out to be a losing strategy. Action, initiated in the mind of the player, takes place at a certain speed (different for every player). Reaction, by definition, has to take more time. And time is a vital ingredient in winning a game.

The default thinking mode in any group of players is — you guessed it — reaction. Thus players have a "natural" tendency to lose unless they are positively motivated to act rather than react.

Boring Lectures: lecturing to the players. Don't do it! For example, if the opposition players are arguing, do not say to your team, "Don't argue." That is lecturing. Boring. Rather say, "You look as though you have the game in hand, team, the opposition players are arguing among themselves." Don't hold the opposition up as an example of what not to do, but use the psychology of looking at the situation from a different point of view. "If the opposition are fighting among themselves they must be very immature and winning will be a pushover . . ." Saying the right thing at the right time can have more effect than hours of lecturing. One short sentence. But you need to think about it beforehand so that you don't say the wrong thing. For instance, if two opposition players argue then some of your players will hear it. On one occasion when I saw this happening I quickly thought about what to do. One of our players was close to me and the ball was not near. I called his name and he looked around. I said, pointing, "The other team are arguing among themselves!" Our player smiled and turned his attention straight back to the game. As he did so he gave me the thumbs-up sign, behind his back as it were. We both knew what he meant. Arguing was forbidden in our team. That sign with his thumb meant we had it won. And win we did. Great communication. No lecturing.

Criticism, Praise and Confidence: never criticise players. Exception: after the game — a long time after — private constructive criticism of the incident rather than the personality of the player, followed immediately by positive comment.

This is difficult for some coaches who believe that criticising the players is their main function! Whether it is true or not, force yourself to think that no player will play badly on purpose. If a player fumbles through lack of concentration — that is the coach's department. If a player is not wholeheartedly enthusiastic about the game — again, that is the coach's field of endeavour. When players look lethargic it may well be something quite different. Anxiety or fear often look like something else; one good player I know looks as though he has a hangover and has been up all night when he is nervous. His play is to hold back, his reflexes look slower and he waits for the opposition to make a move — only then will he move in, usually with aggressive play to make up for the late start. The same player when free from anxiety will move very quickly and dance about delighting in fooling the opposition into moving in the wrong direction. Criticism usually seems to engender anxiety.

Praise. Lots of praise and acknowledgement of skilful play. No insincere flattery. Truthful talking about good bits of play. There are always good bits. Always. However insignificant they may seem when they occur. It is usually possible to say to a player, "You know in the first half when you had the ball right near the side line and you got it past two of the opponents . . .?" And the player will invariably say, "Yes, I remember . . ." A few seconds of action worth praising. The players themselves know when they make bad moves. Going over the bad parts — especially the instant they happen — magnifies the bad. Praise for a clever bit of play produces more good play.

Confidence is the best defence from the Blue Meanies or whatever you call a losing frame of mind. Confidence *can* be induced in a player from such directions as "ball skills", timing, accuracy, perception, anticipation and so on. Every player has something he has done well sometime. Use them to induce confidence. First, determine the limitations of a particular player, say how far or how accurately he can kick. Next, point out to him what he can do. Concentrate on the player by himself, do not compare his performance with another player. Then, with encouragement and praise, point out that whenever he wants to do the particular thing, he can. Making him aware of what he can do while he is practising it is "automatically" building confidence in his own mind. Then when a situation arises in a game that requires him to do something that he knows he has done often before, he will perform confidently.

Dare: encourage risk-taking to sharpen the concentration of players. Taking calculated risks that "come off" is probably the most exciting part of playing the game, after all. Some of the risks will fail but never mind — it's only a game. If they never failed then they were not risks in the first place.

Emotions and Expectations: the basis of the Team System is to manipulate emotions; your own, your team's. By "emotions" what is really meant is the electro-chemical environment in which your brain and the brain of each player operates when playing the game. For instance, when you see something awful you may feel ill, even though nothing physical has happened to you. That is a psychosomatic reaction at a violent level. At a much more subtle level, if you are playing a game and your brain, controlling your limbs, is in a fog of anxiety or fear, usually (not always) your limbs will operate at less than optimum performance. I say "not always" because "quiet desperation" can sometimes produce big results.

The Team System works the other way. First, an environment of joy and freedom from anxiety is created. Then instil in your team a feeling of the expectation of winning. This positive psyching is very "emotional" and is a most powerful force in the world of games. A pass to a player who is moving forward and *expects to win* will be just the correct distance in front of him for his maximum speed — especially if it is being passed to him by a friend. Strategies (even defensive ones) should be worked out with the expectation of winning firmly in the mind of every player. Players who do not expect to win, when moving forward and advancing in the play, will pass almost directly to their team-mates instead of ahead of them. (By "ahead" I do not necessarily mean directly towards the opponent's goal but to where the player will be when he and the ball arrive at the same place at the same time.) A typical case is the back kick. A player with the ball runs in front of his team-mate, but keeps the ball with him. He then does a back pass with his heel. If the player he is passing to expects to win the game he will move forward in a split second and take the ball with him. If he expects to lose the game, he will look at the back pass with surprise, and spend a second or two deciding what to do about it!

Psyching the team to expect to win is completely different from making them feel they *have* to win. You are looking for an expectation and a hope which is not the same as a feeling of responsibility, that they *must* win. You will know that you have succeeded if, when your team loses, they can say, "Oh, well, it's only a game. And we had some fun."

Friendliness and Trust: enforced friendliness is the rule — no arguments or fights are allowed at all. This sounds extraordinary to some people but the effect is worthwhile. A closed society where nobody is allowed to be hostile to another member makes the group a type of club. Every player must know that hostility is forbidden within the team. Only then can he operate in a trusting environment. Once the players feel that security, they will excel beyond all previous limits for the sake of the team. They will run faster, concentrate more, try harder. Players must be told to trust each other and know that, for instance, a bad pass will never be intentional or be from want of trying. Total trust in one's team-mates means that every player can concentrate on his own play. Mistrust means that players are often thinking about other players and that means lack of concentration. If a player cannot reach a pass to him and the ball goes to the opposition he can abuse the original passer — and lose the game. Or he can know it was not intentional, and not think about it further.

Game: not only in training — essential — but also for the game itself, change the players' positions every now and then, whether things are going well or not. A player may well be best in a particular position, but playing in an unfamiliar position does several things. Sometimes players sparkle and shine in quite different roles. A player should know what it is like to play in all positions, to appreciate the other players' situation. It may distract the opposition — a legitimate piece of gamesmanship. This is not always a good idea for the Grand Final but for easy games, for fun games, for friendly games it is a valuable manoeuvre.

Half-time: in situations such as being behind at half-time (that is, your team has a losing score) the psychology used must never produce anxiety. But obviously in such a situation the coach will be anxious! And worried. If your team is losing you feel like a loser. And when you feel that way usually you will lose. So, don't think that way.

Psych yourself first. Think: plenty of teams win after being behind at half-time. But there is a very vital psychology involved in such a situation. It is like this: the opposition are ahead so they will be a bit overconfident. So we can tease them easily . . . the opposition will expect you to be downhearted, losers, timid, and what is the best thing to use against them? Surprise. And the best surprise — well teasing is one. There is, of course, an unlimited number of others. Develop them. They must all be carried out with a plan and they must all use applied psychology in a way that causes the players to take advantage of the fact that they are losing. Some people regard this as lateral thinking (as distinct from the head-on confrontation type). It works remarkably well. Confident winning opposition players do not expect your team to suddenly get tricky. There is your advantage. When one of your players has the ball he can wait until the very last moment and play the ball in an unexpected direction, if possible just out of the reach of the opposition. Unexpected by the opposition, that is.

As a coach — *not* a player — you should know your opposition, know what frame of mind they are in and then manipulate or exploit it. While it is OK for the coach to spend time thinking about the frame of mind of the opposition it is bad news if the players have thoughts that can lead to anxiety. So facts that would cause anxiety should be withheld from the players. A case in point: I was talking to the opposition coach before a game. I expressed admiration for one of his players who was practising. He said, "Yes, he scored a hat-trick last week." I said, "Wow." I thought, I hope our team doesn't hear about *him*. I certainly was not going to mention a word about this superman. So I formed my own one-man conspiracy of silence. What happened? The superman was feeling out of sorts (or something) and played a very mediocre game, a game which we won well. After the game (yes, *after*) I told our players about him. Their comment was that he must have been playing against a particularly poor team to score three goals. And yet when I first heard about him I was inclined to be a bit anxious *myself*.

Now if the opposition are downhearted, then your team can sense it and need not think about them further, except as obstacles to be overcome on the way to scoring. But one of the difficulties a coach faces is lack of information. If your team is down at half-time at least you know one thing — the frame of mind of the opposition and the style of their play. And that is a starting point for your strategy. You are playing against a team that is confident, which often means a team that is vulnerable. Their concentration may fall and perhaps they will relax a little. What you, the coach, are looking for during the first half is a weakness in the opposition, a way through their defences (over, under or around them). Maybe a tactic on the part of your team (like teasing) can surprise them so that mentally they reach a turning point. If they are full of confidence and then suddenly your team scores a goal, the opposition's confidence will probably rate lower than your team's level of confidence.

If a team — the opposition team — is ahead a couple of goals at half-time, it is very likely that they will talk themselves into a *defensive* type of play for the second half. I have heard it. They will expect massive attacks in the second half and they will "batten down the hatches" in a defensive mode. They may place extra players in the full-back positions. Their players may even get in each other's way. That type of defensive thinking means *reactive* play, and reactive play is losing play. (See *Action and Reaction*) So your winning strategy must use your players' brains as well as their bodies. The war cry will be "Action". Generally, if you are winning two to nil at half-time your best strategy is to try for four to nil, not to switch play into a defensive mode.

Internal Competition: have no internal competition. Except perhaps of the children's birthday party type where everybody wins a prize. Some teams operate successfully with intense competition between their own players. But the Team System has none of the kind of competition that can distance players from each other. It is not difficult to have a friendly competition where winners win but the losers are not disadvantaged or discouraged. Now, if this seems silly or unfair, think again. We are talking about a game, not real life.

If your training group is split into two groups, change the players around after every competition so that everybody has the experience of winning — eventually. Then the ones who lose do not become losers in any serious sense. They just become people who did not happen to win that time.

No player should ever feel pleased if his team-mate falls or trips. Sequences like "tackling" another player for the ball should be conducted against another team. Too often have I seen teams training and team-mates really hurting each other. How must they feel when they are passing the ball to a team-mate whose kick still hurts?

If the squad has more players than the 11 required for a game, then no player should spend more than half a game "on the bench". All players should be able to play all situations — such as throwing the ball in from the sidelines — and specialisation (like kicking penalties) should be reduced to a minimum. When there are more players than are needed — for instance many teams have a first team and a reserve team — then the competition between players to make the first team must be of a special type. If a player feels the wrong kind of competition between himself and another player on his own team, then his passes to the other player may have that very small element of just too fast, or just too slow. Imperceptibly, so the competing player will not look quite as good to the selectors on the sideline. And the feeling could be totally subconscious.

The concept of a "team within a team" is seen as a threat by some coaches. When they detect one of these teams they immediately break it up and reposition the players they think are involved. This is sometimes nonsense because the ideal team-within-a-team is not a threat in any way to the other team members. So you will have to decide whether or not your sub-team is good or bad. The members of a bad one will pass to another member of the sub-team rather than make a better shot to another player. The good sub-team is something else. It can be fun to play alongside a good sub-team. When several players form a good sub-team they provide better than normal service to the other players, rather than excluding them. If you are an outsider and you have a good sub-team within your team and you pass the ball to one of their members, they may well do something interesting with it, and that makes *you* look good. If a sub-team does not work well and makes the surrounding players feel "out of it", then break it up. On the other hand, if it does work well and creates no resentment in the team, you may see several players playing as though they had ESP about where their team-mates are without even looking, a wonderful sight.

Joy: if you don't enjoy it, coaching or playing, don't do it! Please. Because my happy team is bound to beat your unhappy team and make you more unhappy!

Killer Instinct: a nasty expression. As a peace loving person I dislike it, but it has one great advantage—in the world of semantics it is commonly understood. In a Grand Prix race you are coming second in your V6 turbo-boosted open wheeler. An opening to overtake the race leader presents itself for a split second. However, if in that split second you hike to 12,000 revs, drop to third gear and *go*, you may not only disadvantage the current leader, but you may cause him to have to brake hard to avoid crashing and harming himself. You know that once you are level with his front wheels then you are the dictator of tactics, you are winning. However, if the previous leader does not handle his new status of coming second and swerves and crashes he may make a widow of his wife or orphans of his children, and that could give you something to think about. If you do think about it, then you do not have the killer instinct, and you will possibly not win. Without the killer instinct you will hesitate, maybe for as much as a whole second. And that's what you will be—second. But the killer instinct in a ball game is not involved with life and death, and if you don't have the killer instinct, you may feel sorry for the opposition goalkeeper. And that is Losing Type Thinking. Cultivating the killer instinct in a soccer game is legitimate. Driving a car on the streets is a good place for totally suppressing it. Totally. You must make the killer instinct a situation-specific thing. In a soccer game it is not only OK, it is highly desirable.

Living Thing: coaching is a living thing. It is not like a formula dealing with inanimate chemicals. It is concerned with living humans. Your players are people. They are chock-full of emotions, some of which are useful in winning a game, some of which can lose the game, even when playing against a poor team.

Making a Goal: teamwork can be strengthened by praising the player who "makes" a goal almost more than the player who scores it. Goal scorers are not more important than any other player on the team, they are (in a way) just the last players to touch the ball, as the goalie might be the first. Goal scorers come in many shapes and sizes. Some strikers have an uncanny sense of when to start sprinting, some have superbly accurate kicks, some have a ball sense that enables them to kick the ball earlier than another player would. Like a Grand Prix driver who sees an opening to overtake, some strikers can kick the ball into the net while other players would still be deciding which way would be best to kick. But they have to have a ball to kick into the net and it has to be in the right place at the right time. The supply line is the goal maker. He sometimes goes unappreciated. Praise him to the skies when he sends in those passes to the strikers.

No Responsibility: responsibility for losing a game should rest with the coach, not the players. Responsibility is a feeling that the players need like they need the Black Plague. It is equally as bad as anxiety. If you asked a person playing a TV game in an amusement parlour if he felt responsible for getting zapped by the spaceships he would look at you strangely indeed. Well, he has the attitude your players should emulate.

Objective: ensure every member on the team knows it is just a game. In fact very few people think it is just a game; most think it is more than a game. A good analogy to use is the TV game one. There is an objective (or lots of them) but it must be a bit of an obstacle course to achieve them — otherwise it would be too easy and no game at all. So the obstacles are the opposition team. That is their only purpose. The game itself is one that your team plays — the game belongs to your team, it is their game — and the aim is to score goals. The opposition team are only there as obstacles to be overcome, after all it would be no fun without them. You could then walk down the field and score without even looking properly! This concept — that the game should not be thought of as your team versus their team in a confrontation contest — is vital. Your team must not think of the game like a boxing match, one winner, one loser. If you, the coach, think of it that way you are sure to convey it to your team, with adverse effects.

Once you have firmly established that you are involved in a game, and that you are playing it for fun, some interesting consequences result. Some things that are bad, even abhorrent, in real life can assume very different aspects when there are no real consequences. The killer instinct for instance, is legitimate in an environment that is specifically non-violent. (Players who play using violence are ordered from the field by the referee.) I do not mean that, for instance, a threatening gesture should be permitted as long as it is not carried to conclusion, not at all. But within the confines of what is agreed upon by both teams as "cricket" and "fair play" interesting situations develop. An example: several times my players reported that the opposing team would abuse our players. Sometimes the abuse — including disgusting references to players' talents, mothers or sexual preferences — sounded almost orchestrated! But it had no observable effect on our players. It did not concern or depress them at all, and at the time I thought it might. Neither did it anger them. Our players repeated to their team-mates what had been said to them and talked about it during the game. But our team stayed completely unperturbed and won. Conclusion: telling your team to abuse the other team would be (a) a waste of time and (b) would take your players' minds off the game. Perhaps that happened to the teams we beat.

Consider this situation: you have the ball at your feet with your back to the sideline and an opponent faces you, crowding you. If you back up with the ball and you cross the sideline, your opponent will have the resultant throw-in. However, if you kick the ball so that it bounces off your opponent's legs and back over the sideline, the throw-in is yours. You have effectively tricked your opponent into "kicking" the ball out of bounds against his will. (And it causes your opponent no pain or injury at all.) This kind of activity in real life and different circumstances might be considered quite immoral. In a game it is just good clean fun. The expression, "It's not cricket" has an English origin and covers the sporting environment regarding "fair play". It means that fair play is understood by both teams and covers situations that do not have to be spelled out. It means that lawyers are not required, that the referee's decision is final, that "foul play" will result in penalties, for example a free kick to the other team, and a player sent off for serious foul play. And within the confines of fair play, there is a lot of good clean fun to be had.

Plan: every player should have a "Next Two Seconds Plan" of what to do if he should unexpectedly and suddenly acquire possession of the ball. He should constantly update his plan. Of course he must be prepared to change instantly his plan and his play if the situation alters while he has the ball. But there is nothing more frustrating (especially to a coach) than a player who suddenly gets possession of the ball, and does not know what to do with it. One of the best ways to sell this concept to the players is to demand of them "their plan" suddenly and often in training. It must be seen as a major failure if a player suddenly gets the ball and then stops to think about what he will do. When players are not actively involved in play and also not moving a lot they must constantly check the position of all other players — both sides. The tendency of players is the same as spectators — to watch the ball and only the ball. While players must know where the ball is all the time (of course) they should also look around as much as possible to observe the other players and their own position in relation to the other players of both teams and the playing field itself. This fundamental fact is often neglected. It is presumed that the only players with anything to do are the ones near the ball, or within its range. Well, in two passes the ball can cover the length of the field.

Quid Pro Quo: means literally one thing in return for another. Think Win versus Think Compensate. To many people Think Compensate is a way of life. "It's an ill wind that blows no-one any good"; "Every cloud has a silver lining"; "Yin and Yang"; "Every action has a reaction"; "Poor little rich girl", etc. Our language is full of compensatory terms. It is considered by many to be a part of nature, that everything that happens has something to compensate for it. Action and reaction are thought of as an actual force of nature, and one that is impossible to avoid. But to Think Compensate is to lose games. For example, I was praising a player after a game for some brilliant play when a bystander said, "Yeah, well that made up for the goal he scored in the first half." Yes, the player had inadvertently put the ball into our own goal and scored a goal against us. The bystander had spoken so that the player could hear him, in fact I think they were friends. I sensed danger. I quickly said, loudly, "Well everybody makes mistakes, but that bit of brilliant play was a joy to behold. Your accuracy was just unbelievable . . ." and on and on. I was forceful enough and carried on for long enough so that the bystander shut up. Thank goodness, I think he got the message. Compensatory thinking is like a poison to Think Win.

There are Think Compensate people everywhere. They cannot help themselves. They call many goals "lucky goals", wins are "lucky wins", and so on. They always, always feel sorry for the underdog. (I think I used to be one.) The best thing to do is not to let them near your team. And if any players in your team are TC people then re-educate them and change them into TW people. It is not as hard to do as you might think. You need to explain the two kinds of thinking and the differences. You need to explain that with Think Compensate thinking you are often thinking of irrelevant things. And the irrelevant things not only do nothing for you but they clog up your brain and leave insufficient room for concentrating on the game. A Think Compensate team tends to relax after having scored a goal. The players feel sorry for the opposition goalie. They think, oh, wouldn't it be just awful to be that goalie and have the ball go past you and score. Poor bugger.

Consider another common situation: you have the ball near your opponent's goal and an opponent accidentally puts the ball into the net — a goal to you. If you have a TC player on your team he will feel very sorry for the opponent (who may be near to tears himself!). Now a TW player on your team will know what the ball was doing there in the first place! The TC players will call the TW player's attitude towards the own-goal-scorer unfeeling, unsympathetic, self-indulgent, uncaring. The TW players will say there are millions of causes worthy of sympathy including the own-goal-scorer — but they (the TW players) are going to postpone thinking about them during the game and particularly while they whoop for joy about the improving score situation. Think Compensate may be appropriate for many situations in real life. In a game of soccer (or any other game) it is death.

Referee: never argue with the referee, and make sure no players do either. Totally forbid it. Some referees have made mistakes, but surely not knowingly. Of the few referees I have known, I do not think that any of them ever made a wrong decision deliberately. And yet in some boisterous spectator crowds opinions are voiced that it happens all the time. In the most confidential moment (where Real Truth is involved) the most any referee has ever admitted to me was that he may have strayed from the path of justice and impartial righteousness against a single player, a violent one. When rough, threatening play has become progressively worse throughout a game, the referee has overreacted and penalised some action which, in isolation, he may have let pass. The decisions have always erred on the side of a clean fair game and against threatening play. Never in favour of evil, as it were.

Humans make errors. And if you think you are right and the referee is wrong—well it could just be the other way around—you could be the one making the mistake. Furthermore there is nothing at all you can do about the referee's decision except get so disgruntled that it puts you (and the players) right off the game. After all, the way to lose a game is to get upset about it.

The solution? Forget about thinking the referee might be wrong. Accept his decision immediately, and get on with the game. England once won the World Cup while the opposition team were arguing with the referee. He had signalled to "play on" and the English team played on while their opponents tried to reason with the referee. The English scored and won. The team should treat each referee's decision as a fact of life, the same as say the width of the goals. If one goal is a centimetre wider than the other—well, who cares? The teams change ends at half-time anyway. Only losers (born or otherwise) spend their time thinking about such things. Losers say things like, "If only the referee had seen the ball touch the opposition player's foot he would have given us the throw-in and we would not have had that goal scored against us and we would not have lost the game and we would have won the championship . . ." and so on. Winners presume that all the rules and conditions will be fair to both teams, bad luck equals good luck in the end, and they "get on with the game". Losers don't, and lose.

Skills: of course you cannot win a game of soccer if you do not have the skills to play it well. Nothing in this book is meant in any way to downgrade or minimise playing skills. And playing skills must be improved with practice, with demonstrations, with coaching, with training. Never let it be said that psyching can win anything by itself. It is obviously never the prime factor in a game, the most important factor will always be skill. But there are few sights more dismal than a demoralised team losing a game. And few more thrilling than a team winning by cooperating with each other, anticipating each other's moves, concentrating, and then maximising their skills by thumping the ball into the back of the net.

Training: training should—indeed must—be as much fun as a game (although it may be hard "work"). Rehearsing "set pieces" should involve every player, with players not directly in the play to act as decoys. After all, if several decoys, say four, are running every which way and one player is playing the ball, the concentration of the opposition is reduced to about half. The decoys are good clean gamesmanship. And teamwork means that the decoys are just as important as the active players. A decoy luring an opposition player into following him is in the same class as a player with the ball moving around an opposition player. It is called the dummy run. A good dummy run is anything but dumb. It is as clever as an Academy Award performance. It is acting in the best sense of fun.

Untruth: never attempt to "con" players by uttering anything untruthful. Ever. Apart from the obvious ethics, a coach who is not believed is of very little value to the players and deserves to lose. This in no way conflicts with my ideas that some things are better left unsaid, and others can be stated with colour and pizzazz.

Visualise: visualise positive moves and go over good pieces of action that occurred. Relive them in group discussion. Act out the action in slow motion with the players who were involved. Point out why it went so well. This is one of the fundamental pieces of psyching (and not only in sports) and the confidence it builds is a very strong influence on good concentration in any similar situation that comes along. It is the ultimate and most fruitful type of post mortem to indulge in. To use it at training is valuable and to use it just before a game is almost essential. On its own, it is one of the most powerful types of psyching. I mean literally on its own. Don't say, "Remember when you did such and such, well do it again today . . ." Just visualise the positive moves with the players. Go over the great action, bit by bit. Don't draw conclusions so much as concentrate on the piece itself. The players will transfer the example to the present situation without being told to. And will do it better than if they are told to. They will get a feeling of confidence out of positive visualisation that is hard to beat. Literally. You are not asking them to do something. You are recalling something that they did. Something good or clever. Not necessarily a winning game or anything big, just something good that actually happened. They did it. If you say to them, "You can do it" you are in the right thinking mode but when you say, "You did it" you are building confidence. If you do it well enough then the players will make the vital connection: "I did it . . . I actually did it . . . I remember doing it . . . I can do it again."

Words: the coach operates in a semantic environment, not one of leather striking leather. And, for the coach, words are more powerful than boots. Words such as "pressure" must be banned or only ever used with a positive meaning. Never "the pressure to win", only "the pressure to cooperate with teammates more, to concentrate more, to run faster, to kick straighter". Never ever "internal pressure". Words like "competitive" have different meanings to different people and to some they can be negative, and to others positive. Avoid such words or say exactly what you mean by them. As coach you are operating in a semantic environment that relates to your team. Everybody in the team must understand everybody else. You do not reach such a situation by lecturing. You have to receive feedback from the players all the time to ensure that your language is within the semantic environment of the team. Words can be a shade more powerful than actions. Which is why some superb players sometimes make poor coaches and some top coaches have not been star players.

"X"—The Unknown: I do not know why the system seems to be unbelievable. The situation stated in the introduction that is, if everybody used the system from this book then all games would be played to a draw — is perhaps true in theory. But the real world is a little different. Not to mention strange.

I was having dinner with the parents of one of my players. It was towards the end of our super successful season, and his mother remarked on what a great job I had done coaching, particularly as I had never played soccer. I had consumed a little wine. Otherwise I would not have said, "It's like this, Ruby. There's a trick to it."

"A trick?"

"Yes. You could call it a trick. And I don't mean that your kid is not a great player. He is."

"What are you talking about, John?"

"Well, by a trick, I mean that the system would work with practically any team. I reckon now I could take any team and show them how to win. You have seen me talking to the team before every game. Bruce (her husband) has heard me."

Ruby looked at me over her glass of wine for a long time in silence. Then she said, "John, you are a good coach and you have a winning team . . . but you are chock-full of bullshit." She was smiling, but she meant what she said.

My immediate instinct was to summon up all my arguments and convince her. I changed my mind on the spot. Instead I said, "Darling, you can see right through me."

"I certainly can," she said.

And that is how it is. I had a few similar experiences and they all ended more or less the same way. Nobody believed me. Well, almost nobody. A couple of friends did, one actually sat in on a few of my pre-game talks and was duly convinced and amazed.

This fact — that it was all so unbelievable — was the prime motivator in my starting to take notes on every game and subsequently compiling them into this book. So the theory of everybody using this system will stay just that — a theory. And if you use the system successfully, don't expect mass adulation. Nobody will believe you! All you will have is the results.

Yell: what do you do when your team scores? Yell your lungs out. Don't sit there smiling. Shout Hooray! You want them to score goals, don't you? Praise clever play (when it has moved away). If you are going to walk up and down the sidelines during the game, be careful. If you (the coach) look or sound anxious when you are calling out, then the players will tend to become anxious. Coaches shouting from the sidelines lose plenty of games, usually because they cannot (no matter how hard they try) keep anxiety out of their voices. If you must shout from the sidelines, make sure you never criticise, that you sound happy and confident. If the players detect stress in your voice, they will quite likely be infected by it. So, if you feel stress, it will almost certainly affect your voice. Keep quiet.

Most important — you must be immediately understood! I have heard coaches call out, "Tighter!" and I am quite sure the players did not know what to do. I have heard a coach call to a player who had the ball, "Take your time" and I watched as an opponent, who was much quicker than the coach anticipated, kick the ball away from the original player. I am sure that player will never take any notice of any similar calls from his coach.

I restricted my calls to "Move out" which was to the full-backs to catch opponent strikers "offside" (this call at the wrong time can bring disaster); "spread out" when players were leaving areas unattended and when more than three players were starting to crowd the ball. Never call out anything that will interrupt the concentration of the players, and never anything that will or can go wrong and make you look stupid! And that is a long list of no-no's. You are not conducting an orchestra or playing with puppets on strings. The players are playing the game, not you. So the most sensible thing to call out is praise, not tactics. The less tactics you call from the sidelines the more the players feel in control of themselves. So work out tactics as far as possible before the game and at half-time.

Zero Anxiety: ensure that the anxiety level in your players is nil. Yes, absolute zero. Never, ever say that the opposition team look good. Ever. No matter how good they are do not talk about them that way. Even if you are playing against Manchester United. Talk about them only in a technical sense — refer to where their players might be and so on. And even then never start talking to your players so that they form an image of powerful opponents. That would mean anxiety. Work this out beforehand. Don't mention two consecutive things about the opposition. Mention one and then get on with the play involved in overcoming or getting around the issue. That is, never chain together aspects like, "Now their strikers are fast and their wingers are very good at passing the ball in to the strikers." That is too much. Do it bit by bit. The fast opposition strikers. How to handle it, not them — the situation, not the players. "Backs come out to catch them offside. Watch if they are onside and they start sprinting . . . be ready to hold fast and force them offside." Space out aspects of the opposition team so that your team can not link two aspects together. If your players start an anxiety loop in their brains they will lose. "Loop" is a computer term meaning it will go round and round in your players' minds and thus reinforce itself and assume greater prominence than reality.

Very important, and worth repeating: never ever say before a game that the opposition team look tough or fast or make any such statement at all. As far as possible prohibit such talk among your players. The less they think about the other team the better. And when they do think about them it should be in a certain way. Make sure your players look at the game like this:

It is your players' game. The only role of the opposition team is to stop your game from being too easy. The opposition must be categorised in your players' minds along with the wind, the sun and the temperature. They are just obstacles and conditions to manipulate.

Conclusion

As stated in the summary, coaching is, above all else, a kinetic discipline. It requires some of that eye-to-eye contact with other humans that is dreaded so much by shy people. (Force yourself — it will be worth it.) It is not a formula where ingredients can be measured and combined to produce a predictable end product every time. In other words it is reactive, depending on the feedback from the team.

For these reasons, the most important factor in the System is to provide the right environment in which (a) to coach the team, and (b) to play the game. Once that environment is firmly in place, then team strategies, group psyching, and responses by the coach to events — especially ones that may never have occurred before — may be developed with some rational plan. Obviously there are many different environments involved here, perhaps it would be better to call them sub-environments. The sub-environments will vary a lot, from intimate, quiet talking, to shouting whoopee on the field to pre-game psyching. But these sub-environments must fit into an overall environment — a framework into which everything must fit without conflict.

My best environment name, without a doubt, was "fun". There may have been different meanings for "fun" in the minds of individual players, but none of the meanings would have been negative. I tend to think a name such as "win" might be dangerous in some circumstances; some players might think it relatively unimportant, while some might think it a matter of life or death, even though in the first place they all agreed that they were there with the common objective — to win.

You do not necessarily need to have an actual name, but you do need to have an idea of the nature of your overall playing environment. And it needs to be discussed with the players. A player who joins a team and does not know the nature of the environment in which he finds himself will often play badly. Witness some First Division transfers of players from one team to another that fail. The transferred player plays badly if he does not fit into the new team. (And the team may have paid a million dollars for him!) While a discussion of playing environment is in progress among yourself and players, be very alert. Override and suppress any contrary views put forward — don't be afraid of contradicting them on the spot. The most dangerous ones to watch for are aggression and fear. And when you have consensus, avoid going into deep psychological meanings. If the players are feeling positive, digging deep to find why they feel that way can often do more harm than good. Everybody sees things slightly differently from one another. What you want to create is a Group Environment in which all your players feel they belong.

In the Team System nothing negative, nothing bad is discussed. And it is the coach who has to publicly prohibit the bad bits such as players criticising other players.

Because the System is a kinetic one, the coach does not have to have a predetermined type of personality. The best coaches in the world do not all look, speak, or behave in similar ways. It does not matter if you are handsome or ugly, big or small. What matters is how you coach your team.

I will not wish you luck, because if you succeed you will make all the luck you need. I wish you success. I also wish you good times and enjoyment in one of the most interesting and rewarding fields of human endeavour . . .

The situation that first gave sense to that incredible concept: that the whole of something really can be more than the sum of its parts. It is called *teamwork*.

BIBLIOGRAPHY

Allen, Louis A., THE MANAGEMENT PROFESSION, McGraw-Hill, 1964.

Bernhardt, Dr Roger and David Martin, SELF-MASTERY THROUGH SELF-HYPNOSIS, Bobbs-Merrill, 1977.

Bettger, Frank, HOW I RAISED MYSELF FROM FAILURE TO SUCCESS IN SELLING, World's Work Ltd, 1951.

de Bono, Edward, PRACTICAL THINKING, Pelican, 1978.

de Bono, Edward, THE MECHANISM OF MIND, Pelican, 1973.

de Bono, Edward, THE HAPPINESS PURPOSE, Maurice-Temple Smith, 1977.

Carnegie, Dale, HOW TO STOP WORRYING AND START LIVING, World's Work Ltd, 1974.

Carnegie, Dale, HOW TO WIN FRIENDS AND INFLUENCE PEOPLE, Angus & Robertson, 1974.

Cohen, Herb, YOU CAN NEGOTIATE ANYTHING, Angus & Robertson, 1982.

Donnelly, Austin, HOW TO PERSUADE PEOPLE THROUGH SUCCESSFUL COMMUNICATION AND NEGOTIATION, Rydge Publications, 1978.

Drucker, Peter F., MANAGEMENT, Heinemann, 1974.

Dyer, Dr Wayne, THE SKY'S THE LIMIT, Granada, 1981.

Dyer, Dr Wayne, PULLING YOUR OWN STRINGS, Thomas Y. Crowell, 1978.

Fearnside, W. Ward and William B. Holther, FALLACY, THE COUNTERFEIT OF ARGUMENT, Prentice-Hall, 1959.

Fersterheim, Herbert, Ph.D. and Jean Baer, STOP RUNNING SCARED, McClelland & Stewart Ltd, 1977.

Fisher, Roger and William Ury, GETTING TO YES, Hutchinson, 1981.

Furst, Charles, ORIGINS OF THE MIND, MIND-BRAIN CONNECTIONS, Prentice-Hall, 1979.

Gittelson, Bernard, HOW TO MAKE YOUR OWN LUCK, Souvenir Press (Aust), 1981.

Gordon, Dr Thomas, LEADER EFFECTIVENESS TRAINING, Wyden Books, 1977.

Heller, Robert, THE BUSINESS OF SUCCESS, Sedgwick & Jackson, 1982.

Heller, Robert, THE BUSINESS OF WINNING, Sedgwick & Jackson, 1980.

Hill, Napoleon, THE MASTER KEY TO RICHES, Fawcett Crest Books, 1965.

Hill, Napoleon and W. Clement Stone, SUCCESS THROUGH A POSITIVE MENTAL ATTITUDE, Angus & Robertson, 1977.

Hill, Napoleon, THINK AND GROW RICH, Fawcett World Library, 1969.

James, Muriel and Dorothy Jongeward, BORN TO WIN, Signet, 1971.

Lorayne, Harry, REMEMBERING PEOPLE, THE KEY TO SUCCESS, Stein & Day, 1975.

Lorenz, Konrad and Paul Leyhausen, HUMAN AND ANIMAL BEHAVIOUR, D. Van Nostrand Co., 1973.

Maltz, Maxwell, PSYCHO-CYBERNETICS, Prentice-Hall Inc., 1969.

Mortensen, Ben F., IF YOU'RE MAD, SPIT!, Brigham Young University, 1978.

Packard, Vance, THE HIDDEN PERSUADERS, Pelican, 1974.

Parsegian, V. L., THIS CYBERNETIC WORLD, Doubleday, 1973.

Peale, Norman Vincent, THE POWER OF POSITIVE THINKING, World's Work Ltd, 1977.

Powers, John, THE COACH, A season with Ron Barassi, Thomas Nelson Australia, 1978.

Rabkin, Richard, STRATEGIC PSYCHO-THERAPY, Meridian Times Mirror, 1977.

Rothschild, William E., PUTTING IT ALL TOGETHER, Amacom, 1976.

Schul, Bill D., HOW TO BE AN EFFECTIVE GROUP LEADER, Nelson-Hall Chicago, 1975.

Schwartz, David J., THE MAGIC OF SELF DIRECTION, Simon & Schuster, 1981.

Schwartz, David J., THE MAGIC OF THINKING BIG, Prentice-Hall, 1959.

Stanton, H. E., THE PLUS FACTOR, A GUIDE TO POSITIVE LIVING, Fontana/Collins, 1979.

Townsend, Robert, UP THE ORGANISATION, Coronet Books, 1970.

Wagner, Abe, THE TRANSACTIONAL MANAGER, Prentice-Hall, 1981.

Weekes, Dr Claire, PEACE FROM NERVOUS SUFFERING, Angus & Robertson, 1972.

Zimbardo, Philip G., SHYNESS, WHAT IT IS, WHAT TO DO ABOUT IT, Addison Wesley Publishing, 1977.